PROFITING
FROM
INNOVATION

National Academy of Engineering Study Committee on Profiting from Innovation

William G. Howard, Jr.,
  Chairman
Robert A. Charpie
Philip M. Condit
Robert C. Dean, Jr.

Richard E. Emmert
Joseph G. Gavin, Jr.
John W. Lyons
William F. Miller
Harold G. Sowman

Bruce R. Guile, *Study Director*

PROFITING FROM INNOVATION

*The Report of the
Three-Year Study from the
National Academy of Engineering*

William G. Howard, Jr.
Bruce R. Guile
EDITORS

THE FREE PRESS
A Division of Macmillan, Inc.
NEW YORK

Maxwell Macmillan Canada
TORONTO

Maxwell Macmillan International
NEW YORK   OXFORD   SINGAPORE   SYDNEY

The Free Press
A Division of Macmillan, Inc.
866 Third Avenue, New York, N.Y. 10022

Maxwell Macmillan Canada, Inc.
1200 Eglinton Avenue East
Suite 200
Don Mills, Ontario M3C 3N1

Macmillan, Inc. is part of the Maxwell Communication Group of Companies.

Printed in the United States of America

printing number

2 3 4 5 6 7 8 9 10

Library of Congress Cataloging-in-Publication Data

Profiting from innovation: the report of the three-year study from
   the National Academy of Engineering / William G. Howard, Jr., Bruce
   R. Guile, editors.
        p.   cm.
     Includes bibliographical references (p.   ) and index.
     ISBN 0–02–922385–7
     1. Technological innovations—Management.   I. Howard, William G.
   II. Guile, Bruce R.   III. National Academy of Engineering.
   HD45.P76   1992
   658.5′14—dc20
                                                            91–25638
                                                                 CIP

Contents

v

Preface and Acknowledgments

In 1967 the Secretary of Commerce, John T. Connor, convened an advisory panel of technical business leaders and charged them with considering the impact of taxation, finance, and competition on invention and innovation. That panel, chaired by Robert A. Charpie—who was then president of Union Carbide Electronics—wrote an excellent and widely read report titled *Technological Innovation: Its Environment and Management*, "the Charpie Report." It is worth quoting the featured recommendation of that report, a recommendation considered by that panel to be more important than any specific recommendation concerning antitrust, regulation of industry, or financing of innovation:

> The major effort should be placed on getting more managers, executives, and other key individuals—both in and out of government—to *learn, feel, understand* and *appreciate* how technological innovation is spawned, nurtured, financed, and managed into new technological businesses that grow, provide jobs, and satisfy people.[1]

The intervening years have given the world a growing body of work on technological innovation and invention, but the problems and concerns raised by the Charpie report are by no means solved. The last two decades have taught us that some U.S. companies are good at managing some aspects of technical innovation for profit but that many are weak at developing and applying new technologies and converting those technologies into businesses. This has been brought home to us by growing international competition that has made foreign steel, automobiles, consumer electronics, semiconductors, and production equipment as common as, or more common than, those products made domestically. It is hoped that this book can help move us in the direction of that 24-year-old recommendation —to make a contribution to the knowledge of managers and executives about how technological innovation becomes business success.

On behalf of the National Academy of Engineering, I would like to thank the study committee for this project for their time, energy, and dedication in preparing this book. The committee members William G. Howard, Jr. (chairman), Robert A. Charpie, Philip M. Condit, Robert C. Dean, Jr., Richard E. Emmert, Joseph G. Gavin, Jr., John W. Lyons, William F. Miller, and Harold G. Sowman gave generously of their time and experience. Bill Howard, the committee's chairman, served during most of the study as a Senior Fellow of the National Academy of Engineering and his contribution deserves special thanks. I would also like to thank the study director, Bruce R. Guile, for his efforts and constancy of purpose in bringing this project to fruition.

The study committee was aided in their deliberations by a much broader community of individuals involved in technical and business matters. I would like to extend the Academy's thanks to the people who participated in and contributed to two wide-ranging workshops held as part of the study process and to an unusually large number of individuals who gave their time in reviewing drafts of the book manuscript. In addition, several members of the staff, past and present, of the NAE Program Office deserve thanks. In particular, Jesse H. Ausubel, Bette R. Janson, H. Dale Langford, and Hedy E. Sladovich all made important contributions to the project. Finally, I would like to acknowledge the financial support that allowed the NAE to mount and complete this project. Long-term program funds provided by the NAE's many 25th Anniversary Fund contributors were crucial to this project, as was a special grant from the Hewlett-Packard Company Foundation. Naturally, the interpretations and conclusions in this book are the study committee's and do not purport to represent the views, positions, or practices of any funding organization.

ROBERT M. WHITE
President
National Academy of Engineering

PROFITING
FROM
INNOVATION

1

Why This Book?

*M*any company leaders are blind to the potentials, pitfalls, and day-to-day challenges presented by technical change. Managers, financiers, and entrepreneurs generally appreciate the value of experienced management, an educated work force, abundant low-cost capital, a good location, or a recognized brand name. They are often less comfortable with technology, too often regarded as simply "R&D" or "patents." Most managers regard technology as important in some undefined way, but not as pressing a concern as meeting next month's sales targets or structuring the company so that it is unattractive to hostile takeover artists. This attitude, bred of a lack of sophistication about the uses, management, and pervasive effect of technology on the structure and competitive environment of business, can cripple a company.

Profiting from Innovation is intended to help managers make informed judgments about managing innovation to add value in a technologically dynamic world. It is meant to help company leaders make better decisions about investing in or managing technologies that can add value to products, processes, or services. The focus is not necessarily on producing new or technologically advanced products, processes, and services, but on ways of effectively applying and managing innovation for profit. The goal of using technology in business is not just technological excellence, but business success. Such business success may arise serendipitously from a truly new technology, but more likely it will follow from a focused program of technical and business work and from making improvements to existing products and processes faster and more effectively than competitors.

Microelectronics, gene splicing, computer communications, and efficient airfoil design are technologies pregnant with possibilities. It is, however, the products that result from their application that produce business success. These technologies have spawned a host of new products and services, such as personal computers, bioengineered pharmaceuticals, networked computer applications, and jumbo jets, that could not have existed 25 years ago.

Often the range of products and services that incorporate such new technologies quickly grows beyond the capacity of a single firm to exploit. With rare exception, knowledge that products based on a technology are market successes spreads quickly and belongs to the world almost immediately— knowledge that a technology is effective in production diffuses only a little more slowly.

This forms an important baseline for thinking about managing technology: *Static monopoly of a given technology and its applications is unsustainable in the long haul*. As disconcerting as this may be, it is important to realize that there is no safe or permanent success in technological or business matters. Success is only the opportunity to compete in the next round. Thus, the challenge of profiting from innovation lies in understanding how to transform new ideas efficiently *and* routinely into marketplace advantage—in mastering a dynamic process.

Profiting from Innovation seeks to encourage business success in two ways. First, it is an introduction to four patterns for incorporating innovative technical ideas in new products, processes, and services. It also discusses management practices that are important in creating the drive to use technology effectively. A key to realizing the business potential of technology lies in understanding the nature of commercialization processes—their driving forces, pace, risks, and impact. Technological advance is not separable from its uses or from the organizations, people, and markets it affects. Managers and entrepreneurs must understand the complex web of interactions between technology and people, markets and organizations. They need to know where their products, processes, and services fit technologically and in the market, the best way to structure and prosecute commercialization activities, and how internal capabilities can be used to match external opportunities. *Profiting from Innovation* provides a basis for harnessing innovation by describing the nature of several types of commercialization activities. Knowledge of when specific commercialization activities are under way and understanding the characteristics of those activities are important elements in effective commercialization management. This is not exclusively, or even predominantly, an issue for high-technology industries. It is as true of the paper clip business as it is of microelectronics.

Second, *Profiting from Innovation* will help a manager or entrepreneur recognize and act on opportunities for adding value, opportunities that differ at various stages in the life of products, processes, and services. At the outset, value lies in the search for applications and means, and the benefits come from being early to market. Later, value comes from executing product, process, quality, or service improvements sooner than others do. Still later, value comes from correctly managing maturity. As simple as it sounds, there are many ways to be distracted. We will discuss tools and techniques to help managers keep on track and not lose sight of commercialization goals in the confusion of day-to-day activities.

The insights, ideas, and analysis in this book can provide an alternative to what some business observers have called the triumph of paper over product. In his 1989 book *The Resurgent Liberal*, Robert Reich, a scholar and prominent critic of U.S. business strategy, drew the following distinction:

> Paper entrepreneurs—trained in law, finance, accountancy—manipulate complex systems of rules and numbers. They innovate by using the systems in novel ways: establishing joint ventures, consortia, holding companies, mutual funds; finding

companies to acquire, "white knights" to be acquired by, stock-index and commodity futures to invest in, tax shelters to hide in; engaging in proxy fights, tender offers, antitrust suits, stock splits, leveraged buy-outs, divestitures; buying and selling notes, junk bonds, convertible debentures; going private, going public, going bankrupt.

Product entrepreneurs—inventors, design engineers, production engineers, production managers, marketers, owners of small businesses—produce goods and services people want. They innovate by creating better products at less cost; establishing more-efficient techniques of manufacture, distribution, sales; finding cheaper sources of materials, new markets, consumer needs; providing better training of employees, attention-getting advertising, speedier consumer service and complaint handling, more-reliable warranty coverage and repair.

Our economic system needs both. Paper entrepreneurs ensure that capital is allocated efficiently among product entrepreneurs. They also coordinate the activities of product entrepreneurs, facilitating readjustments and realignments in supply and demand.

But paper entrepreneurs do not directly enlarge the economic pie; they only arrange and define the slices. They provide nothing of tangible use. For an economy to maintain its health, entrepreneurial rewards should flow primarily to product, not paper.

Yet paper entrepreneurialism is on the rise. It dominates the leadership of our largest corporations. It guides government departments and agencies. It stimulates platoons of lawyers and financiers. It preoccupies some of our best minds, attracts some of our most talented graduates, embodies some of our most creative and original thinking, spurs some of our most energetic wheeling and dealing.[1]

Our focus is on exploiting technological opportunities for organizing design and production activities, and for encouraging innovation in design, creation, and delivery of products and services. The object may be making potato chips or microchips, package delivery or management consulting, sorting checks or producing toasters. A central theme of this book is that profiting from innovation requires management preoccupation with running the heart of the business, a pre-occupation with the business, operational, and technical matters that allow a company to make a better product or provide better service less expensively.

Strategies that are primarily financial—acquisitions, mergers, divestitures, and strictly tax-motivated invest-ments—are important aspects of business, but they are not our focus, except as they affect the ability of a firm to develop and deploy technology for business growth. Instead, *Profiting from Innovation* has a great deal to do with technology and engineering management in industrial settings.

The central message of this book is that commercializa-tion is a complex process. There are no simple prescriptions to enhance effectiveness. Management's goals and tech-niques must vary with the characteristics of the technology, the maturity of the technology, the requirements of produc-tion, and the parameters of competition in each industry. This diversity forces flexibility in management approaches, techniques, and strategies. Obvious truths, perhaps, but ones often lost in cookie-cutter approaches to business manage-ment that tend to treat industrial biomedical research, pro-cess innovation in financial institution back offices, and new materials use in automobiles as simply "innovation." For a manager to select appropriate methods, organizations, ex-pectations, and even tools for tracking progress, he or she must understand the true nature and complexity of the ac-tivities involved. A superficial understanding will not do.

It is important to acknowledge at the outset that this book draws very heavily on the experiences of the study commit-tee and those who joined the committee for two workshops (August 1988 and January 1989) and on scholarly work in the area of the management of technology and the economics of technical and industrial development. This book would not have been possible without individual contributions of managers and engineers from a wide variety of industries and earlier scholarship on innovation management. The ref-erences in text are meant to convey the depth and breadth of the existing and emerging literature in the areas treated in this volume and to acknowledge the debt that this manuscript owes to a large and growing community of researchers and practitioners in this field.

Finally, a word about the intended audience for this book. The six chapters of this book cover many basic concepts and examples in relatively few pages. That approach was dictated by a desire (1) to demonstrate a few fundamental insights about the parallel processes of technical change and business development; and (2) to launch managers, engineers, entrepreneurs, and students in directions leading to profit from technological innovation. Experienced managers and technical professionals reading this book—on their own or as part of management training courses—should find enough "real world" experience to convince them that many of the ideas and suggested approaches can be of immediate practical value. They may recognize many of the points from their own professional experience. Faculty and students in business and engineering schools should regard this book as the starting gun for a longer race, an overview, teaser, and perhaps framework for what might be covered in a comprehensive first-year graduate course in the management of technology in business. At a reading time that clocks between five and ten hours (depending on reading speed and coffee breaks), the book is designed to be read in a couple of sittings—one transcontinental flight if you are fast and two afternoons at the campus library if you are inclined to savor your assigned reading.

2

The Prepared Mind

Understanding Technological Innovation in Industry

Fortune favors only the mind that is prepared.

LOUIS PASTEUR

*E*very business participates in technological change as an originator, user, or victim of technological invention and innovation. Managers who understand how they participate in the process of technological change have a powerful advantage, especially if they recognize and pursue innovation as a process of company renewal. All are equally uninformed about the future. But since many technological business opportunities are wagers against uncertain futures, fortune is likely to favor the leader who is aware of current trends and opportunities—one who has a prepared mind.

The first step toward understanding technical innovation in industry is to recognize that technology and business structures evolve together—sometimes slowly and sometimes quickly. The development of electric motors and that of dry document copiers illustrate the period and character of much commercial technological change.

7

The electric motor arose in 1873 in a form most of today's consumers would have trouble recognizing. Early electric motors were extremely large—very large horsepowers—and applied first to electric railways. This early application prompted the solution of complex problems of generation, distribution, and application of electric power. Slowly, electric motors moved into industrial systems. In 1894, 21 years after invention of the motor, the first all-electric factory was built in the United States. Particularly significant was the way that electric motors allowed the distribution of power sources to different machines.

A central engine with physical power links between engine and machinery was the norm in steam-powered or water-powered factories. By applying electric motors it became possible to decentralize the application of power in a different way.

The period between 1900 and 1910 may well have been the decade of the electric motor. Production of electric motors more than doubled with predominant applications of this dramatic new technology in iron and steel mills, elevators, electric vehicles, and fans.

The spread of electric motors continued as the number of applications grew and motors became cheaper and smaller. In 1930 a Harvard Business School professor estimated that of the 28 million households in the United States, 8.7 million had vacuum cleaners, 6.7 million had electric clothes washers, 5.9 million had electric fans, and 3.0 million had electric sewing machines. Today the electric motor is just about as pervasive a technology as can be imagined. Razors, toys, subways, computer cooling fans, and robot arms rely on electric motors. The U.S. motors and generators industry sold over $7.5 billion worth of equipment in 1990 and employed tens of thousands of people. Today's American home could easily have 100 electric motors. Many are smaller, more powerful, or more ingeniously used than they were just 25 years ago, and the number of applications continues to grow.

Copying documents—today regarded a human need, not a technology—has seen a variety of technological changes, as illustrated by this excerpt from an article by David Owen published in *The Atlantic* magazine:

The first office copiers were, as is well known, monks. When Gutenberg invented movable type, in the early 1400s, monkdom trembled. Some time afterward the Abbot of Sponheim wrote a lengthy treatise arguing that monks "should not stop copying because of the invention of printing." To ensure that his treatise got the readership it deserved, the Abbot had it printed. A couple of hundred years went by. In the mid-1600s someone pressed a moist piece of tissue paper against a written document, causing some of the ink of the original to transfer to the tissue. A couple hundred more years went by. Blueprints were invented in 1842. Typewriters, carbon paper, and mimeograph machines were introduced a few decades later.

Carbon paper and mimeograph machines were improvements over hand copying, but neither could be used to reproduce documents that already existed. Mimeography, furthermore, was a terribly inefficient way to make a small number of copies, since each document required its own master. Schoolchildren love mimeograph copies, because they smell so terrible, but almost everyone else hates them. Photostat machines, which were introduced in the early 1900s and which make copies photographically on sensitized paper, were much too expensive for ordinary office use. They were also too big, too slow and too hard to use. When a businessman needed a copy of something, he generally called in the functional equivalent of a monk.

This didn't really change until the middle of our century, 500 years after Gutenberg. . . . Office copying as we know it didn't arrive until 1960. That year a small company in Rochester, New York, began marketing its Haloid XeroX 914 Office Copier (the second capitalized X is a flourish that the company later dropped). The 914, unlike its competitors, made good, permanent copies on ordinary paper. The machine, though large, was simple enough for a child to use. Haloid Xerox, Inc. had been marketing a small number of machines employing its revolutionary copying technique for a decade, but the 914, the first model intended for general office use, was also the first to catch on in a big way. The number of copies made in American offices grew from around 20 million in 1955 to 14 billion in 1966 to eleventy zillion today.[1]

These examples are useful because they show the way in which the evolution of technology can happen slowly even as fortunes are made and lost. The electric motor history stands in contrast to the stories of business success in the videocassette recorder, computer, or semiconductor industries, where incremental advance has happened very quickly. The copying history illustrates that the two patterns—rapid and slow change—can and do coexist.

At any given time it is possible to identify overlapping or nested technological changes. A technology may become viable in new products and markets (the way fractional horsepower motors moved into household appliances after considerable diffusion in industrial settings), or a product market may be marginally changed by substitution (nylon used instead of metal for moving parts in a kitchen drawer assembly) or dramatically changed by a new technology (jet engines replacing propeller engines in airplanes). The intersection of a particular technological advance and a particular set of market conditions occurs, however, in a predictable pattern, a pattern that can determine the challenges to companies operating in affected businesses.

The shared development of technologies and industries has been explored by scholars of business and technological history such as Rosenberg[2] and Chandler,[3] and it is from this work, as well as more popular business and technological literature, that one can gain insights about the patterns of technological change. The essence of a prepared technological manager is the ability to recognize and distinguish among the various ways in which technical change provides opportunities and pitfalls for businesses.

DISTINGUISHING
COMMERCIALIZATION CHALLENGES

While there are few strict rules, technologies and industries do tend to evolve in consistent patterns that, if perceived even dimly, can help a manager chart a profitable
course in use of technology. Management consultants, technical professionals in industry, and scholars of technical
change and diffusion have done substantial work on understanding patterns by which industries and technologies
evolve together or how management approaches need to be
sensitive to the character of technological development.[4]
While there is no widely accepted formal model, there seems
to be agreement—if only tacit—that important and pervasive patterns do exist.

The most widely shared model is based loosely on growth
curves and product or technology life cycles. Figure 2–1
shows a simple yet powerful model of many growth processes. The S-shaped or logistic curve—which plots a growth
in numbers over time—can be used to model applications of
a successful new technology in the marketplace, giving us a
primary model of penetration of technology. The absolute
values for a particular diffusion curve (elapsed time and
sales) are related, of course, to the specific nature of the
technical change and to the scope of the change. The nature
of progress in each phase of the growth curve is strongly
affected by the drivers of progress. Understanding these drivers and the nature of processes they provoke is an important
clue for effective commercialization management.

This simple S-curve pattern is widely used in the study of
the diffusion of technical innovations. It can be applied both
to major, long-term changes, such as the growth in air transport, and to the life cycle of a single product, such as a particular generation of a particular company's personal
computers. This simple model allows us to identify and discuss four patterns of commercialization that occur during
the emergence, diffusion and development, and maturity of
technological advances.

Figure 2–1 Technology and Business Life Cycles

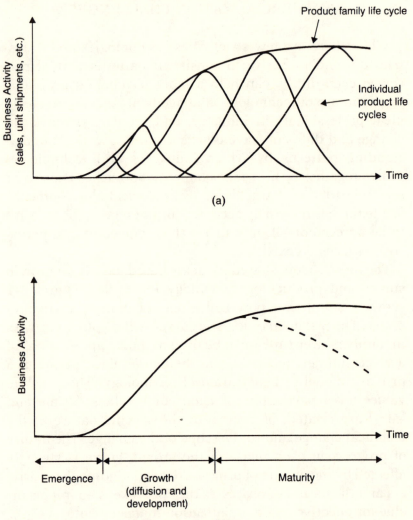

(a)

(b)

(a) The life cycle of a business consisting of a family of products is the sum of the life cycles of family members. (b) This life cycle is an S-shaped logistic curve consisting of three distinct phases; emergence (the development of the product or service, its manufacturing capabilities, and its place in the market), growth (where the product family pervades the market), and maturity (where the market is saturated and growth slows).

Emergence: The emergence of a product or process is characterized (1) by genuine technical novelty; or (2) by the use of a previously developed technology in a new market application. In either case—whether it is new technology pushing into the market or the market pulling an existing technology into new applications—this period in a technological development is likely to be a period of great ferment as inventors, developers, and users carry out a trial-and-error search for applications that work.

If the new product, service, or process arises from technical novelty, there is likely to be a much greater variation in the nature of the product, as competition is often based more on product or process characteristics than on price. We will call such truly new products or processes *technology-driven opportunities*. The challenge in such technology-push cases—many of which begin with a serendipitous discovery by scientists or engineers—lies in finding market applications and manufacturing means for the new technology.

New products, services, or processes that arise from a perceived market opportunity—those which involve the use of fairly well-understood technologies in new marketplace settings—can be characterized as *market-driven opportunities*. The challenge in these market-pull situations is in the search for the best technology, whether in-house or external, and the process of mutual adaptation between market and technology as a company "works" the technology to fit an untapped demand and thereby create a business.

Although commercialization efforts always involve elements of both technology push and market pull, it is important to understand the primary driving forces, since effective management techniques for these two activities can be very different. In either case, emergent commercialization activities usually entail more uncertainty, both with respect to technology and market acceptance, than found in commercialization later in the life of a product or process family.

Diffusion and Development: The rise of a dominant design (or application that meets the requirements of the marketplace) speeds the pace of diffusion and changes the nature of competition. As diffusion proceeds, price competition becomes more important (there is less differentiation based on product characteristics). The pure economics of production and delivery dominate competition in a way that they did not in early stages. These *product- and process-improvement opportunities* permeate "high-tech" businesses and are present even in mature industries.

Maturity: When the pace of technical change slows in a particular application, the product or service becomes ripe for innovation. The established technology becomes mature in application and in danger of being replaced. This is an *end-game opportunity* where businesses face uncertainty about the values and risks inherent in further investment in an existing and mature set of products or processes, seeking replacement technology, or abandoning the field.

Each type of commercialization opportunity demands tailored management approaches—best approaches to organizational structure, management tools and techniques, investment criteria, the competitive environment, elements of risk, and decision criteria.

TECHNOLOGY-DRIVEN COMMERCIALIZATION

Truly new technology creates a few important markets for the patient, lucky, and smart (and often small) business units.

Though basic science is not often the immediate source of a firm's commercial success, technological or scientific discoveries can create new market opportunities. Pharmaceuticals or other industries where innovations can be effectively protected by patents or trade secrets are an important exception. Industrial innovation has a special character when new science, or serendipitous technological discovery without any new scientific knowledge, creates market opportunities. At early stages of the development of a truly new product or service, there is real technological

competition—it is a race between those pushing improvements in existing technologies and others bent on developing the power and usefulness of the new technology. During
this period, inventors and users carry out a trial-and-error
search for applications of an initial idea that works—both
technically and in terms of consumer acceptance. In the early
1900s, buggy makers competed with car manufacturers for
market, and car manufacturers competed with each other in
the search for a superior product design and production process.

Rarely, however, is a technology revolutionary. Usually in
technology-driven development, the change is an evolutionary application of existing or emerging engineering knowledge to a new product or service. Early in the 1950s,
technology for piston engines for large aircraft reached a
high level of sophistication, just before being washed away
by turbine-based jet engines and turboprops. It was a fierce
competition for evolution of the older technology (piston engines) until inexpensive, high-performance, reliable new
technology changed the standard of performance for aircraft
propulsion.

In technology-driven efforts, when a new product or service is not yet tried in the market, there are usually few
participants. A company's success may depend on visionaries who see something that others do not and are willing to
risk a great deal to pursue it.

*Among the many examples of successful technical entre-
preneurs are Arthur L. Fry and Spencer Silver, who developed Post-it Notes at 3M. During one of 3M's open-ended
research drives, Silver had stumbled on to an adhesive
that would stick, but only lightly and which could be re-
positioned without losing its tack. According to Silver,
the new tacky substance resulted from "wanting to see
what would happen." But what was the new substance
good for? When Silver showed his new glue to others, he
found they lacked his excitement, mainly because he
could not tell them how it could be used. As a result, Sil-*

*ver had to wage a personal battle within 3M just to
patent his new product.*

*Silver believed this unique product had to be useful,
and he continued to tout his adhesive to every division
of 3M until he finally convinced the Commercial Tape
Division to seek product applications for it. The division put a team together to find a use for Silver's glue.
One member of the team, Arthur L. Fry, was always
bothered by the clutter of errant bookmarks in his
church choir hymnal and he found that if a small
amount of Silver's substance was applied to each slip
of paper, the bookmarks would remain where he placed
them until he wanted them moved. This realization began the chain of events that led to Post-it Notes (considered the most pervasive office supply breakthrough
since transparent tape).*

*"It was some private quality . . . that motivated Spen-
cer Silver. . . . Silver was not the problem-solver who figured out what to do with the adhesive. . . . But he knew
there was something special about the stuff, and he
shopped his little vials of glue around the corporation for
five years. People took turns turning him down, and
everybody got a chance—until he finally caught the attention of the right person." Without Silver's persever-
ance and determination to find a use for his adhesive,
and 3M's tolerance for tinkering and acceptance of the
extraordinary, the Post-it adhesive would have gone
uncommercialized.*[5]

The idea of value to the customer lies at the heart of new
product and service development; technologically new products that are successful can be more expensive than older
products, but the services they deliver are "better" in a way
that justifies the price. Such was the case with instant photography, automobiles (which transported people and goods
at greater cost than horse-drawn vehicles or trains, but more
conveniently), pocket calculators (which initially did little

more than the much less expensive adding machine and slide rule), dry copiers (which were more expensive than carbon paper), and computer-automated medical imaging equipment (which cost far more than conventional medical x-ray equipment). The same is often true of process innovations, which may initially add production cost but end up increasing quality, decreasing environmental impact, or allowing more flexibility in response to customer demand.

Management Challenges: The management challenges in tapping markets and using new processes created by new technologies occur in at least three distinct areas. First, a company must generate (or capture), recognize, and evaluate truly creative technological ideas. The history of new technology markets is full of stories about smart and lucky "inventors" turned down by successive layers of management or backers.

Second, a company must be able to handle the technology —to execute on the promise of an idea. This means envisioning a product or process application, determining a sound plan for further development of the technology, executing that development, managing scale-up, and technological adaptation based on early and often hard-to-read feedback from the marketplace.

Third, a company often has to be willing to create a market or an application for a technologically new product, service, or process. Although some new products seem to leap to the marketplace (or, in the case of process innovations, into use), many more must be coaxed and coddled to succeed. Potential buyers have to be convinced that the product or service will work as expected; complementary technologies must be developed and made cost-effective; and standards must be established and accepted. The technology must meet a demand; and the company must have the ability to deploy products and services that match customer needs.

In most technology-driven commercialization cases, the biggest risk is market acceptance, as illustrated in Robert

Lucky's description of AT&T's attempt to bring video to telephone service:

> The Picturephone® was a celebrated development of the Bell System in the late 1960s. It was a personal irony for me that when I took a course in "managing innovation" during this period, the development of Picturephone® was used as a case study of a "perfect" technological development. It met schedule and cost objectives, while overcoming a series of significant technical obstacles. Unfortunately, it was soon to be discovered that there was more to life than successful technology.
>
> The Picturephone® was introduced as a product in 1971, primarily in Chicago, with a monthly price of about $125. Market studies had, of course, been done to predict its acceptance and growth. The mathematical model of the predicted market growth was similar to that of a contagious disease—you did not want to be the first to get one but after a certain number of your friends got one, you would be likely to jump on the bandwagon. Thus it was predicted that the market would start slowly and then after reaching a certain level, would take off. This prediction turned out to be half right.
>
> In retrospect there were a number of difficulties or mistakes in the Picturephone® debacle. Some people say the price was too high, or that the black-and-white Picturephone® came out at a time when people were expecting color, or that the resolution was too low. These observations are undoubtedly true, though probably in themselves not the reason for the market failure. My own belief is that the Picturephone® offered too little benefit to human communications to justify the awkwardness and technological intrusiveness of the instrument.
>
> The Picturephone® failed because the market—society's need—was seriously misjudged. It was a case not only of mechanically incorrect market projections, but of a lack of fundamental understanding of the true societal nature of communications. These issues are deep and murky, and not amenable to simple technological solutions. It even took the ordinary telephone several decades to gain acceptance from a wary public.[6]

MARKET-DRIVEN COMMERCIALIZATION

Latent markets create opportunities for commercially important technological innovation using existing technology (that is, necessity really is the mother of invention.)

Most new commercial applications of technology are not developed as a direct and immediate result of the discovery of new scientific knowledge. Technology often emerges from crafts and skills, building on existing technology even when there is no new scientific knowledge involved. People often discover and invent things based on prior technological art, without understanding the fundamental science.

In most cases, therefore, the primary driver of commercialization is the realization that a need exists for a new process, product, or service. The nature of the commercialization activity is a search for the best technology to meet an identified need.

A technology can be applied in several different product or production equipment markets. Sometimes application of an existing technology to a new market is dramatic, for example, the application of video tape recording (used in commercial settings starting in the late 1950s) to home television-oriented entertainment rapidly spawned new product and service industries. In other cases, efforts at moving existing product and service lines into new markets are more incremental, and the technological challenge is in packaging and applying an existing technology so that it matches the characteristics of the target market.

These are nontrivial technical challenges. As with product- and process-improvement developments, there is no substitute for knowing what the customer wants, but the challenge is similar to that in technology-driven developments— envisioning how customers will respond to a product or service that does not yet exist.

Bell & Howell's Publication System Division, which developed an electronic automotive parts catalog for au-

tomobile dealership repair facilities, provides an excellent example of market-driven commercialization. The base for their market entry was a history of publishing microfiche for library and other reference use and an aggressive "airplane research" activity that allowed them to assemble and build a sophisticated system of real value to users with "off-the-shelf" technology.

In the 1980s at the suggestion of General Motors, Bell & Howell set out to modernize the automobile parts catalog. Bell & Howell faced the challenge of creating a product that would process a large volume of data and improve response time and electronic image quality. This required addressing five critical management and policy issues. The most important of these was analysis of customers' needs, accomplished through customer surveys, focus groups, and one-on-one interviews. The second central issue was one of a willingness to apply new technologies to meet market needs. This resulted in generating leading-edge technologies, including infrared touch screens, gray-scale monitors, optical-disk storage devices, and networking. Management's persistence was the third important factor. For more than 10 years, despite failures and mounting costs, management was flexible enough to respond to market feedback and engineering experience. The fourth factor was a corporate philosophy of encouraging progress through innovation. For example, annual interdivisional technology conferences provided a forum for examining technology trends and presenting new product concepts. Strong project management was the fifth factor. To develop new electronic equipment and cope with resource requirements on an unprecedented scale, management reorganized the division, relocated the entire team in nearby but separate facilities, and implemented classic project management processes refined for specific needs.[7]

Management Challenges: Market-driven cases may not be dependent on home-grown technological responses to market needs. Finding and using the best available technology—wherever it resides—to create a new business is the critical activity. The challenges to management look very much like those of creating an application for a technology-driven product or process, but with the added concern that a company is much less likely to have a proprietary position in a technology. Choice of technology and time to market may make all the difference. Successful management of market-driven commercialization therefore lies in compelling a firm to be a successful "hunter-gatherer" of technology to meet a demand in a market not already served.

A strong relationship with customers can be a special advantage in pursuing a new market with existing technologies. Customer loyalty—a willingness of potential buyers to share the risk of experimentation because of a track record of performance in a previous technology—makes a big difference.

The dominant challenge in market-driven commercialization lies in identifying and applying the most appropriate technological solution to market and manufacturing demands. When a firm fails in pursuing a new market with an existing technology-based product or service, the failure is often the result of making the wrong technological choices, or moving slower than the competition to the marketplace.

PRODUCT- AND PROCESS-IMPROVEMENT COMMERCIALIZATION

Technological competition in product and process improvement is the bread and butter of industrial technological innovation.

Once a concept using a new technology has been proven in the market, competition quickly shifts to quality, price, performance, and features, with less competitive emphasis on fundamental differences in product or service characteristics. Often a dominant design or application emerges that meets the requirements of the marketplace, and new competitive factors arise besides technology-based product and service characteristics.

The typical pattern is illustrated by medical computer-automated imaging equipment, overnight package express, and automated banking teller services that were, as recently as 1975, new and different products. After one or two initial marketplace successes, competitors swarmed in quickly and the focus shifted from making it work once to making it work to make money. Within 15 years, these items had become standard offerings, and early providers and later entrants now engage in competition over incremental improvements · in the product or service—competition over market expansion and market share rather than over market creation. Bacon and Butler recognize this pattern, even in a relatively mature industry:

> In such instances, a small increase in technical performance of the product may have great commercial significance. For example, the Hogan Golf Company was able to reduce the total club weight less than 10 percent while maintaining the same swing weight with its "Legend" shafted clubs. The commercial result of this relatively small technological improvement enabled Ben Hogan to more than triple their sales in three years and move to number one in sales of golf clubs by pro shops.[8]

The pace and character of market development (technological diffusion) depend on a variety of technological and economic factors not related directly to the product or service. At the most general level, these technological factors are part of "the system" that surrounds a product or service. For example, steam-powered locomotives awaited development of steel rails before railroads would grow. The automobile would have remained a specialty item were it not for the creation of standardized parts and the moving assembly line. The facsimile machine boom relies on the telephone system; the videocassette recorder depends on the universal use of television sets, the ability of Hollywood to provide enough product, and at least a limited degree of standardization. The same is true of industrial products. The growth of polyester fiber for all kinds of uses depended on the development of a commercially viable process for making terephthalic acid, an important feedstock for the production of polyester.

Technologically based products and services evolve as part of a changing structure, and most products or services are either behind or ahead of the system with which they must merge. This issue arises most clearly in markets where standards—both technical standards and marketplace "common use" standards—become both a constraint on the possible applications of technology and a central battleground for competitors. For example, operating systems and interconnect standards currently play an important role in the evolution of computer and telecommunications markets.

A drive to create universal computer communications capability has led to the development of "Open System Interconnect," or OSI standards, which provide a common basis for computers from diverse manufacturers to communicate with one another. A universal communications environment provides opportunities for new producers to participate in a rapidly growing market by simplifying the ability of their products to interact with a variety of previously installed equipment.

On the other hand, installed base—the extent to which a provider has customers committed by prior investment to continued use of his products—can be an important factor in establishing a distinctive competence for that provider. For computer interface standards, IBM's proprietary interface standard, Systems Network Architecture, or SNA, is the most widely used computer communications protocol. Customers with an existing network of IBM computers have a strong incentive to expand by buying more IBM computers rather than risk data interchange incompatibilities.

Similar considerations apply to a variety of other product fields where investment in spare parts inventory, tooling, and training provide important incentives to continue with past purchasing selections. The commercial airline industry is an important example—maintenance, pilot training, and ancillary equipment needs are all simplified by standardization of a particular company's fleet of aircraft.

As a product, process, or service approaches maturity, the market begins to be saturated and new applications and new markets give way to a replacement of previous generations of the same type of product or service. At this point the challenges change and increase. The demand for power hand tools, wheelchairs, and hotel services seems to have reached this stage. There are terrific opportunities for technological innovation at this stage, but they come from pushing improvement—new materials, new designs, and changes in fabrication or delivery. Life insurance policies are old products, but today's ability to offer rapid rate quotation or claims processing depends on the ability to manage nationwide, or even global, communications networks. Construction design and engineering have been around for millennia, but the 1990s have brought a new technological challenge to construction engineering firms in the use of computer-aided design tools for improved engineering quality, faster design cycle time, improved customer communication, and reduced cost.

Figure 2–2 shows the rapid drop in the price of computer memory and, as such, illustrates the way in which a technological product can change with time. This can strain a company's ability to push continuous, incremental technological and organizational innovation in production, an ability that is crucial during periods of rapid market growth. Since production-driven commercialization is characteristic of much industrial activity, continuous improvement skills are important to a wide range of enterprises.

It is important to recognize that, as this stage of development proceeds, the cost of a significant technical improvement rises as the costs of research, development, and production process improvements increase and the technology begins to reach its practical limits. Exploiting technological advance after the initial market success of a

Figure 2–2 Average Price of Computer Main Memory Byte

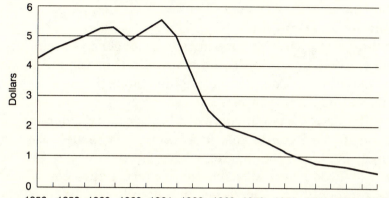

SOURCE: After K. Flamm, *Targeting the Computer: Government Supported and International Competition* (Washington, D.C.: Brookings Institution, 1987), p. 215.

technology-based product or service can be like the second squeeze of a lemon: There may be plenty of juice left, but it takes more effort to get at it. In some cases, relatively expensive parallel development strategies may be necessary.

This parallel development path strategy is particularly evident in the evolution of the dynamic random access memory (DRAM) semiconductor integrated circuit business. Companies that were ultimately successful leaders in this fiercely competitive product area had as many as three generations of product under development simultaneously. As the 64K DRAM was entering production in 1978, the 256K design was beginning commercial product design, and a 1Mbit future product was the subject of intense R&D efforts.

Companies that adopted a serial product and process design philosophy, focusing all efforts on a single product generation, were kept continually off balance by a procession of new products reaching the marketplace in quick succession. They found themselves asking how their rivals developed products so rapidly. The answer turned out to be simple—successful producers were not faster at developing new products, but rather they started earlier, and invested in parallel development projects.

Successful DRAM companies took longer to develop new products, so they could invest the time required to debug new products thoroughly before the rush to market began in earnest. The cost of not pursuing simultaneous developments was that serial development projects were continually in a reactionary mode, rushing products to the market, often before they were ready. Products reached customers before they could be thoroughly characterized and often had to be recalled for design modification. Customers got the impression that the serial developers did not understand what they were doing.

There are, of course, exceptions to the typical pattern—industries that rarely move out of the technology-driven stage of development. In these industries, a single company can establish and maintain a strong proprietary position. The pharmaceutical industry, for example, is one in which a strong proprietary position is far more important, over most of the product cycle, than production costs. The technological aspects of competition in pharmaceuticals occur almost exclusively in the research laboratory and in product development, testing, licensing, and patenting.

In general, however, the most drastic mistake a manager can make is to assume that there is no improvement—technological or otherwise—that can be made in a product or process. Putting such a conclusion in print, as did the *Scientific American* in January of 1909, is almost foolhardy: "That the automobile has practically reached the limit of its development is suggested by the fact that during the past year no improvements of a radical nature have been introduced."

Speed and quality of incremental innovation are critical to success of product- and process-driven commercialization efforts. Ralph Gomory, former senior vice president of IBM for science and technology describes the "cycle" of product development:

> Most development work is done just one step ahead of manufacturing. While the company's plants are making the 256K chip, R&D is working on designing, refining, and processing the 1-megabit chip. When the 1-megabit chip is ready, manufacturing ramps up, increases volume—and the 256K chip is phased out. This triggers development work on the 4-megabit chip so that the process can start all over again. This pattern appears in all kinds of manufacturing—cars, consumer electronics, jet engines.
>
> One cannot overestimate the importance of getting through each turn of the cycle more quickly than a competitor. It takes only a few turns for the company with the shortest cycle time to build up a commanding lead.[9]

The need for speed in commercialization does not lessen the need for care in executing all the tasks needed to bring a product to market or a process to the production line. False starts, where products introduced to the market must be called back to correct design or production flaws are usually worse than being late. Instead, emphasis on speed of execution means using those planning, goal-setting, and organizational techniques that help the project to progress.

The fact that time is of the essence in product- and process-driven commercialization efforts focuses attention on the cycle speed in an organization. Being the first to market new products or to employ improved manufacturing processes enables the developer to participate in potentially the most profitable part of the product life cycle. Ability to complete the commercialization process more quickly than the competition provides a powerful capability to keep opponents off balance through improved product features, lower cost, and improved quality. As Gomory observes, this effect compounds with repeated cycles.

During the 1980s there was a significant resurgence of interest in production and design/production/customer-service relationships. This has been, in part, a reaction to the perception that foreign manufacturers, the Japanese in particular, had become substantially more productive than their U.S.-based competitors. As a result, "good practice" has begun to change. There is an important and growing literature on such things as design for manufacturability, statistical process control, just-in-time systems of manufacture, simultaneous engineering, and organizational design for effective customer service. Attention to these topics has been heightened by the growth of computer-aided design and computer control of manufacturing processes, which create potential for increased electronic control of production systems.

This book cannot do justice to what is a vast and rapidly evolving set of insights about what makes for effective management of production operations. What is common among the emerging practices and literature is a commitment to virtually continuous improvement in all aspects of production, whether that relates to communication between product designers and manufacturing operations or to the way a unit process contributes to the performance of a manufacturing line. Increasingly it is recognized that if management is not willing to regularly allocate resources to continuously improving material transformation (manufacturing) or operations, a company will not successfully be able to bring new products and services to market. This is a stark change in attitude from the recent past when manufacturing operations were not regarded as amenable to significant improvement; in many companies the production process was regarded as something to be squeezed for cost savings rather than managed for improvements in effectiveness.[10]

Management Challenges: Continuous product and process improvements do not just happen—they must be driven by the expectation that such improvement is the basis of future competitive advantage, and must be eagerly sought if the firm is to succeed. Laurence Seifert suggested several simple rules to guide the development of automated manufacturing.[11] Slightly modified, they are excellent rules of thumb for the manager leading product and process improvement:

- *Do not accept performance as it is.* Make yield-improvement, quality, and failure-mode analysis a major, constant activity.
- *Don't just do the same thing a bit faster (or cheaper, or automatically).* Continual, careful reexamination of product and process designs is essential to product and manufacuring improvement.
- *Learn to deal with people's natural reluctance to accept change,* as typified by the following commonly heard complaints:

  "There's nothing wrong with our manufacturing processes; the problem is the product designers."
  "There's nothing wrong with the product design; the manufacturing people are just not competent to make it."
  "We can't afford to spend time and money on productivity (training) programs."
  "We already have too many engineers."
  "We simply need to get labor rates down."
  "If only the product forecasts were more accurate!"

Managers must relentlessly encourage improvement in every aspect of the business. They must measure their performance with respect to competitors in terms of the rate at which they introduce improvements to the market (cycle time), the rate at which they make improvements as production volume expands (as measured by the experience curve), and the degree to which the entire work force contributes to improvement.

The motivation for technology-based incremental improvement in the performance or function of an existing product or service can arise from customer demands or from the opportunity to reduce production costs or improve quality. Traditional market research can be an "arm's-length" way of judging customer sensitivity, but reliance on such indirect understanding can easily lead well-intentioned efforts astray. Many design engineers have never talked to users of the product they design, and many corporate managers who have never visited customer locations have lost touch with the real needs of customers.

Creation of a "customer first" culture in a company requires corporate leadership, and business structures and practices, that bring customers into direct and continuous contact with the people designing, producing, and maintaining products or services. Practices for knowing and understanding the customer will take hold only if improvements in the quality of the product and the efficiency of the production process are regarded as important. There are always opportunities for more efficient and higher quality production, and it is management's responsibility to pursue them relentlessly. In product- and process-improvement commercialization, the biggest challenge is surpassing the competition.

Finally, time is a crucial factor in the success of technological products and services. Being the first to enter a market with either a new product or the next upgrade of an existing product family can create tremendous advantage, especially if leading the competition is a perennial accomplishment. A company that delivers the next small improvement in a product or service will have a small advantage over the competition, but a company that delivers 10 small improvements ahead of the competition is likely to create a great advantage. This corporate capacity—the ability to deliver a continuous stream of incremental improvements to the customer—is invaluable in most competitive arenas.

END GAME

Business maturity and technological shifts create special problems and challenges.

With mature products, in which potential gains are design and production driven, a tension arises inside companies between (1) an unequivocal commitment of resources and management attention to product and process improve-

ments despite slow market growth and (2) a decision to
maintain the business line with low reinvestment to allow
resources to be available for developing and deploying new
products or services for new high-growth markets. Maintenance, while seemingly the safe course of action, can be very
risky as mature products and processes are candidates for
obsolescence due to major changes in product and production technology. Few established companies can rise to the
challenge of the major discontinuities in their business base
that arise from revolutionary technology changes.

The business world is littered both with those who grew
complacent and did not invest in improving a product perceived to be mature—the "cash cow"—and with those who
stayed too long with a superseded product or service. To cite
just a few examples, the shift from horse-drawn buggies to
automobiles, from piston aircraft engines to jets, and from
mechanical to electronic timepieces all left more than a few
companies behind. Discontinuities of technological
advance—the shift from one technology to another—call for
visionary focus. Commitment and successful negotiation of a
technological discontinuity may depend on a deep understanding of, and commitment to, the end user.

A well-honed organization, aimed at producing an existing
product or service efficiently, may not be able to muster an
effective response to significant technological change. Usually the routines and practices of a mature organization work
against a new idea—individuals pressing on new ideas are
not easily accommodated by a mature organization, autonomous power and high financial rewards are not easily ceded
to those who would pursue a new approach. The right visionary leadership—either from top management or at lower
positions in an organization—must lead a company through
significant technological change.

In his classic study on Beretta, the Italian arms maker,
Professor Jaikumar notes the need for significant organizational change at each discontinuity in arms manufacturing
technology.

*The history of arms manufacturing encompasses six
clearly defined production epochs, and as many as 80 percent of original firms were unable to adapt and failed to
make the transition between epochs. What is important
in understanding this case is the production consistency
in the circumstances of these six epochs as they were experienced by Beretta. (1) Each epochal change represented an intellectual watershed as to how people thought
about the manufacturing problem. (2) Most of the gains
in productivity, quality, and process control achieved by
Beretta in its 500-year history were realized during the
assimilation of the six epochal changes and very little in
between them. (3) Each epoch entailed the introduction
of a new system of manufacture: the machines, the nature of work, and the organization all had to change to
meet a new technological challenge. (4) It took about 10
years to assimilate the change incurred by each epoch.
(5) Every change represented the solution of a process
control problem whose process variance was perceived to
be highest. (6) All of the changes were triggered by technology developed outside the firm.*

*It is obvious that each of the epochal changes affected
all of the metal-fabricating industries. What is important
is how changes in each of these epochs affected process
variance—the measure of "out-of-controlness" that a
process is designed to contain—and how the reduction of
this variance led to a science of manufacturing.*

*The six epochs represented attempts to tackle specific
problems in the management of system variance—
accuracy, precision, reproducibility, stability, versatility,
and adaptability. The first three epochs—the English,
American, and Taylor systems—related to the material
world of mechanization. Each saw the manufacturing
world as a place of increasing efficiency and control,
substitution of capital for labor, and progress through
economies of scale. These objectives were obtained
through an engineering focus on machines and what
could be done with them. All of the next three epochs can*

be described as introducing a new industrial order, where the intellectual leap is made from mechanization to information processing. These epochs were (1) statistical process control and the dynamic world, (2) information processing and the era of numerical control, and (3) intelligent systems and computer integrated manufacturing. All three brought a reversal of the trends of mechanization: increasing versatility and intelligence; substitution of intelligence for capital; and economies of scope. Machines came increasingly to be seen as extensions of the mind, and as meant to enhance the cognitive capabilities of the human being. The versatility of information technology and freedom from mechanical constraint suggested a new management imperative.

Though Beretta originated none of the major metal-fabricating innovations or new approaches to information processing in work, it was quick to adopt every one of them.[12]

In firms with a single product line, a major change in technology can bring many outcomes, ranging from business failure to a revitalized company-wide focus on a common effort—developing, making and selling, and delivering a new product or service.

Companies with several major businesses face a different problem. A decision to balance a product or service portfolio often calls for building some businesses while harvesting others. Strategies that turn successful, mature, slow-growth businesses into cash cows to feed newer, more attractive "stars"[13] can be dangerous. Those who work in mature, profitable operations find it easy to forget the importance of quality and winning in the marketplace, to feel left out of corporate efforts to move forward technologically, and to settle for coping. A business decision to treat a product or service line as mature may doom the product line to extinction.

Management Challenges: Companies in technologically mature businesses—the end game of a business—face a continuous balancing act. Too little attention to an existing and apparently mature business can allow less established competitors to gain market share. Some industries, on the other hand, do disappear in the face of technological change, and some business lines must be phased out—buggy whips in 1910 and vacuum tubes in 1965, for example. The management challenge is to guard against *overcommitting* to a new and growing product line that can make existing businesses look pale and lifeless in comparison. It may be appropriate to regard a mature business as a source of cash for other business ventures, but it is important not to underestimate the value of an established business and so give up on the growth potential of a mature business prematurely.

Managers of mature businesses face a series of critical decisions, the outcome of which can have a profound effect on their company's future. The first decision calls for forecasting whether the current product or production technology will be supplanted by new, substantially better technology. If yes, the options are to try to embrace the new ways, or to exit the business before the new technology destroys the old and to apply the resources to other, more promising activities. Where technological replacement is not predicted, a shakeout of competitors is likely as the product family matures. Management choices in this case are whether to exit early, while the product line retains its value, or to persist to the very end when only a small number of suppliers dominate the business, with commensurate cash-generation possibilities. Companies that elect to persist, but are unable to, are often the losers, as their exit must take place at a time when the residual value of the business is minimal.

A balance must be created between the new and the old; both call for attention and resources. On the one hand, new products look exciting and the real uncertainty of growing a new business can be overshadowed by "greener pastures" forecasts of potential markets. In practice, of course, significant investment in product R&D, process R&D, and market development is likely to be crucial to make ideas profitable in practice. On the other hand, the old business probably has

a large infrastructure of both R&D and business unit operations, and it can be easy to spend large amounts on R&D
and new capital to squeeze out the last few increments of
improvement possible, increments that may never yield an
adequate return.

A decision to treat an operation as a cash cow should be a
conscious, considered decision and fully communicated as
such to the entire organization. Allowing the mature business to stagnate by lack of attention is the surest way to lose
quickly the revenue generated by the business. Management
must set challenging goals for all functions in the operation;
marketing, production and manufacturing, engineering, and
R&D. It must be made clear that a focus on quality remains
a high priority and that some cash cows have long lives in
competitive markets and can be as rich and potentially profitable as the hottest new technology product. Benchmarking
(to be discussed later) is particularly valuable in maturing
industries to evaluate the capabilities of the company with
respect to others in the business and to establish reasonable
and achievable targets.

Finally, a company should never relinquish entirely the
core technological capability that accompanies an active
business. This provides ability to solve problems that will
inevitably arise and to do low-level technology-based
searches for process (and less often product) improvements.
In a mature business a company can signal to competitors
and users that management believes in the potential of the
business by maintaining a significant core set of technological capabilities.

THE RANGE OF COMMERCIALIZATION CHALLENGES

Using the four patterns described above, it is possible to
understand and analyze the vast majority of technological
innovations in industry. The following observations describe
some of the changes over the course of the business life cycle
(both past and future developments):

- Some truly new technology-based products and services are refined and developed by being tested in the marketplace.
- Technological evolution is an important part of every product or service business during growth to maturity. Technological changes can be rapid and incremental, and management must relate those changes to an evolving system of production and use. Substantial technological advance is likely to become much harder and more costly over the life of a product.
- Well-developed but still evolving technologies are constantly creating opportunities for entry into markets served by products and services that are based on other technologies.
- Increasing efficiencies of various kinds accompany production and consumption growth as users and producers become more familiar with the underlying technology. This, however, comes at the cost of increasing "stiffness" in the system as standards and installed base grow. This can create a barrier to revitalization or replacement with services and products based on different technologies.[14]
- Mature product and service markets exist in a tension between further improvement along an existing technological trajectory and the shift to a new trajectory and possibly to a new set of producers of goods and services.

These loose, overlapping models of industrial technological innovation, challenges, and processes provide a taxonomy of the process—a structure useful in asking fundamental questions about the best approach to profiting from innovation.

Although *technology-driven commercialization* occurs rarely, it is a particularly important part of total commercialization activity, for "orthogonal" innovations do not follow logical extrapolation of business growth. When successful, technology-driven products, processes, and services can produce extremely large and rapid business growth for either start-up companies or existing businesses. Such technology-driven advance can also make the competition's products and services obsolete.

In contrast to the conventional wisdom that a better a mousetrap will sell itself, management challenges—not inventiveness—dominate in technology-driven commercialization. Effective commercial exploitation of a truly new technology requires a special skill and luck at finding a good market fit between technological opportunity and customer demand and then deploying a product or service that effectively uses the technology and meets the demand. In some cases, the skill and luck are directed by external pressures such as government regulation or a competitor who obtains a particularly dominant patent position.

The special and uncertain character of truly new technological opportunities means that few, if any, businesses can depend principally on technical revolutions. They occur infrequently, entail a level of risk that makes them a hazardous foundation for most businesses, and rarely provide the sustained push that a company must have to endure in the market marathon.

Market-driven commercialization challenges lie in managing the matching and fitting process that brings the resources and opportunities of a reasonably well understood technology or set of technologies to bear in a previously unexposed market. The hunter-gatherer skills necessary to be successful at many of these challenges are different from those for other types of commercialization. While there is room in market-driven opportunities for technological visionaries, comparative advantage is most likely to arise from customer contact or special, often well-developed, technological competence. Penetration of new markets with existing technologies requires either deep technical competence or existing and ongoing connection to the market that a company is trying to penetrate.

Product- and process-improvement commercialization is frequently the heart and soul of technology-based competition in modern markets. It often requires the capacity to manage a growing organization and to be competitive at producing products and services of higher quality and usually faster than the competition. It is perhaps perceived to be a less exciting technological opportunity, but it is the one of greatest consequence for companies and managers. Product- and process-improvement commercialization is the basis for day-to-day competition in established businesses, and is therefore the primary factor in overall industrial success.

The *end game* presents its own set of management challenges, but they are challenges of judgment and investment. Am I betting my company's future on buggy whips or electric motors? If the buggy whip business disappears, can I get into steering wheels and accelerator pedals? If demand for electric motors persists, do I have the resources to hold on, develop new product evolutions, and gain market share sufficient to support a company through a period of low-margin business while my competitors decide to chase some new type of motor? Is it perhaps best to sell the division and simply buy shares in an assortment of blue-chip companies?

The next chapter examines ways of getting an analytical handle on management challenges pushed forward by technological change and the special requirements of managing technology effectively for profit.

3

Management
Tools and Techniques

*If a hammer is your only tool, all problems begin to
look like nails.*

ANONYMOUS

*U*se of organizations to exploit the profit potential of new
technology—to understand and cope with variations in
the character of technological advance—is both art and science. The art reflects a certain "feel" evidenced by an ability
to see ahead—usually based on knowledge, imagination, and
sensitivity to change. The science involves the use of formal
or informal analytical tools to understand and prosecute the
commercialization process and to motivate action. Analytical tools are a means to sift through disorganized data to
grasp commercialization issues. "Rules of thumb" based on
such tools provide the decision framework. They can help a
manager cope with confusing facts, competing ideas, limited
funds, and looming deadlines.

The driving force behind a search for effective tools is a
sense of restless disquietude about company performance.
This feeling should manifest itself in the following probing,
almost personal, questions about the business:

- How do my products and process technologies compare
  with those of others?

- Are new ideas appearing in my competitors' products sooner than in mine?
- Are my new products and services timely?
- Are projects proceeding according to my plans and expectations?
- Are new processes easily set up?
- Is my product and process development cycle time shorter than that of others?
- Are my products accepted by consumers and recognized as high-quality, high-value products when *first* introduced to the market?
- What can I do to improve product and service acceptance and minimize performance failures that hurt sales?
- Are the cost, quality, and functionality of my products better than those of my competition?
- Have other companies been commercially successful with opportunities that my company identified but could not bring to market?
- How do individual functions, and teamwork between functions, in my company compare with the world's best practitioners of those activities?
- What are the next steps to be taken to improve?

These are general driving questions. Analytic tools, suited to specific occasions, can help a manager grasp their answers. Some, such as financial decision-making and operating tools, are widely used because they are universally understood. Other tools, more specific in their focus, are applicable to particular commercialization situations. Analytical tools help managers separate meaningful information from the confusion that surrounds commercialization activities.

Analytical methods such as experience curves, product life cycles, competitive analyses, benchmarking, decision and risk analysis, discounted cash flow analysis, technology forecasts, and milestone charts help decision makers organize, operate on, and filter information to obtain an ongoing image of the project as it develops. Depending on the situation, some tools are more useful than others for keeping projects on track and making an activity work toward a profitable outcome. Such tools, however, do not substitute for more detailed understanding. Tools are at best rules of thumb that indicate when and where to look further at operational details to gather information needed for decision making. Rules, as the saying goes, are made to be broken, and these analytical rules of thumb are no exception. They are merely indicators to prompt further attention.

What follows is a short catalog of analytical tools that have proven to be helpful in many cases. The list is by no means complete—it is intended as a beginning for thinking about commercialization assessment. No such catalog of analytical indicators can ever be comprehensive; there are many ways to look at a business. Each basic principle can be applied in different ways to diverse business activities—it is up to managers to adapt the basic idea to meet specific needs. Adaptation of analytical tools requires the same kind of originality shown by engineers in selecting and tailoring technical tools and procedures to solve specific design problems. The techniques need not be elaborate, but they must provide useful information matched to business constraints and success factors. One example follows:

A manager of an integrated circuit design department found that he was confronted by more product development opportunities than his department could handle. The primary limit to expansion of his business was technical support required for the development of new products. Improving return on this technical investment was an important goal in his use of available assets. In such a manufacturing business, this meant generating as much profitable manufacturing activity as possible given his limited development capability.

New product opportunities ranged from high-volume, low-priced commodity products to application-specific products that sold for high prices, but in small quantities.

The manager observed that 5 percent of his product line's sales income went for development engineering. Since reasonably accurate estimates of development cost and eventual sales volume for the product opportunities were available, he used a ranking of development cost divided by sales as one of his selection indicators. If the return on development investment was 20:1 or better, the return on the most limited resource improved. Other indicators, such as profit on sales were also useful, but ranking opportunities by return on development costs provided the basis for making best use of the available resources.

The ranking technique was only the initial screen for evaluating product opportunities. Many other considerations could override the ranking of return on development cost (for instance, collateral business with the same customer, experience with promising new markets, or need to counter product offerings by other companies), but ranking provided a framework for decision making. The lower an opportunity's position in the ranking, the more compelling these additional reasons had to be to override the basic rule of thumb.

Choice of business indicators can significantly alter strategies in a business. Emphasis on long-term growth in market share as a primary measure of business success, for instance, can produce a business strategy that is very different from a plan for the same activity based on short-term profits, or return on investment.

In the same way, different analytical tools can produce quite different pictures of commercialization activity. A given project must be subjected to a number of diverse tools to obtain an accurate picture of its progress and prospects. Tools to be used must be adapted to the specific type of commercialization at hand and to the stage of product conceptualization, development, manufacture, and market maturation. More complete and formal analytical tools may be used as product commercialization reaches more advanced stages; valuable tools for projects driven by product and process improvement may be quite inappropriate for technology-driven or new-market-driven cases.

MEASURING WHAT MATTERS AND UNDERSTANDING THE COST OF NOT ACTING

One start-up company CEO characterized the process of innovation as consisting of the following steps: Market need—Fanatic entrepreneur—Invention—Money—Chaos— Proof of principle—No money—More Chaos—More money—Commercial success or personal failure.

Financial project analysis and management budgeting and accounting practices pervade all commercialization activities. With regard to new business creation, it is no coincidence that small company CEOs frequently cite insufficient financial backing, and the eventual consequences of not obtaining financing, as their most significant problem. Project or start-up financing problems may not be as obvious for commercialization projects in large companies, but return on investment nevertheless plays a crucial role in their ultimate fate.

Financial success (and demonstrating its likelihood at the outset) is crucial to successful commercial technological innovation. Though commercialization champions may need to focus on technological, market, and organizational challenges, the investment that drives advance requires a payback, a return.

The logic of project finance is inexorable and sound— current and future returns, adjusted to reflect the time value of money, must exceed investment. The problem arises in applying the simple, tight logic of financial analysis to decision making about technological issues in real companies, involving matters of great uncertainty, using information provided by less than neutral parties to the decision.

Take, for example, the decision to proceed with development of a technologically new product for an undeveloped market. Setting aside technological issues, calculation of return on investment for the product and market development expense still requires estimates of the following:

- The cost of developing a prototype.
- The cost of manufacturing a product for which neither a prototype nor a manufacturing line exists.
- The market for, and likely sales of, a product that does not yet exist over the next several years (remembering that the product must be priced at a sufficient margin above a manufacturing cost that is not yet known).
- Other uncertainties about such things as the long-term (and often not yet perceived) environmental effects of manufacture, use, and disposal and the potential liability exposure of making and selling the new product.

Underlying the uncertain and often fuzzy judgments that must be translated into numbers for financial analysis are fundamental questions about the technology and the technological capability of the company. Will the technology work? Will it meet consumer demand? Can the people in the company develop it faster than the competition?

With regard to product and process improvement, management accounting practices often determine the data collected and most analyzed by company decision makers. As such, accounting practices usually create the context in which decisions about a company's technology are made. It is easy to see how business information systems can be badly designed and managed for technology development and application. Budgeting systems, for example, and systems for attributing costs are flawed if they arbitrarily place research in department A, technology acquisition in department B, development in department C, product prototypes or process experiments in department D, and manufacturing in yet another department. The processes of creating and using technology are more complex than the model implied by such a budget-driven organization. The development and use of new technology should be seen as a system with the flows and feedbacks required to make it work, though individual parts may be separately managed day-to-day. Often the accounting and planning information used for decision making does not reflect a true picture of technology, products, and production. As Robert Frosch, vice president, General Motors Corporation, put it:

> It was precisely at that point in the history of computation when it became easy to track even the most complicated inventories item by item that the Financial Accounting Standards Board went from first-in-first-out to last-in-first-out accounting for inventory control. From a production point of view, both accounting conventions are misleading and offer no guidance on how most effectively to manage production.[1]

Commercialization activities should be based on the task at hand, not on peripheral considerations. The challenge of business information systems is to build meaningful links between research, development, outside technology acquisition efforts, product design, and production *as appropriate to the current, pressing challenges*. Information flows, both formal and informal, must reflect tasks on the critical path of development.

Project financial analysis and management accounting techniques *can* be valuable in translating operational and planning considerations into the general business context. Figure 3–1 shows several often-used financial tools, some of which are of great value in managing technical enterprises. Their apparent precision, however, must not blind managers to the limited accuracy of the underlying assumptions and data. Decisions based on differences of a few tenths of a percent of discounted cash flow are of questionable value when the assumptions are accurate to plus or minus 50 percent. Financial analysis is often too blunt an instrument for evaluating technological opportunities—it cannot deal with the breadth of business problems that managers confront.

Given the uncertainty of the process, it is a wonder that any manager ever considers financial analysis of corporate technological matters. But all decision makers do look at financial calculations, probably because there are no other

Figure 3–1 Financial Measures of Company, Business Unit, or
Project Performance

Measurement and tracking of the financial performance of operations are crucial in management and decisions. A variety of financial tools are available to help analysts and managers determine current levels of performance and to translate expectations into current value for decision making. Simplified versions of three types of financial measurement techniques are described below. Each is valid, but they provide only a partial, and sometimes too weak, basis for decision making about the development and commercialization of technology.

1. Profitability ratios measure returns generated on sales or investment, often in comparison with industry standards. The following are common ratios:
   a. Profit Margin on Sales = Net Profit After Taxes / Sales
   b. Return on Total Assets = Net Profit After Taxes / Total Assets

2. Activity ratios measure the uses of resources and are best used in comparison with industry standards. Four typical measures are the following:
   a. Fixed Asset Turnover = Sales / Net Fixed Assets
   b. Total Asset Turnover = Sales / Total Assets
   c. Average Collection Period = Receivables / Average Sales per Day
   d. Inventory Turnover = Sales / Inventory

3. Project evaluation and comparison methods help to select among competing uses for funds. They are particularly important to commercialization decisions, as new products or processes are often easily conceptualized as the implementation of a project. Two common methods are the following:
   a. *Payback method* calculates and compares the time to pay back initial investments for project alternatives. The more rapid the payback, the more desirable the project. The payback period is the time it takes a company to recover its original investment from net cash flows from the project.
   b. *Discounted cash flow method* finds the present value of expected net cash flows of an investment, discounted at the cost of capital. Net-present-value and internal-rate-of-return project evaluation and comparison are types of discounted cash flow analysis. The advantage of these approaches is that they account for both the company's marginal cost of funds and the time profile of expected returns.

tools so pervasive. Most managers understand basic financial tools in the abstract, and that makes them the coin of the realm no matter how inappropriate their application.

Finally, a serious problem in applying financial tools to company technological matters is their inability to evaluate the eventual costs and consequences of *not* acting. A decision not to take an action can be as serious as a resolution to proceed. The tendency to view commercialization activities as financial burdens, instead of means to seize business opportunities, introduces in management thinking a subtle bias against reach-out efforts. As George Bernard Shaw put it, "You see things; and you say 'Why?' But I dream of things that never were; and I ask 'Why not?' " This holds for management: the intangible cost of not acting to meet future needs must be considered as well as the tangible costs of proceeding.

In rapidly changing technologies, for example, failure to invest in future product or process improvements provides openings for competitors to undermine a company's market position. Assessing the cost of not acting entails understanding the promise of yet undeveloped products and processes and how, if introduced to the market by a competitor, they would affect existing, as well as future, business. The cost of not acting may be to deny forever the opportunity to compete, since the cost of catching up may well become prohibitive very rapidly. According to Donald Frey, former CEO of Bell & Howell:

> Success or failure in technological business is a contingent matter. Much of what determines the success or failure of commercialization of an innovation is beyond the control, and often beyond the scope, of the business organization. Survival of a new product or process is contingent on such uncontrollable and unknowable forces such as customer desire for an undefined product, the economics of a new process in use, the state or development of supporting technologies, or the math skills of a customer company's work force. The typical practice of discounted cash flow analysis deals with these contingent conditions either poorly or not at all. Discounted cash flow, internal rate of return, or net present value techniques—all the same thing with different names—are particularly unable to tell you the consequences of not doing something innovative; the tool is ill suited to the task and its recommendations should be regarded with suspicion by managers who want to succeed at commercialization.[2]

In short, the cost of not acting must be as important a part of evaluation of future options as the age-old question: "How much will it cost?" Continual evaluation of options is essential if one is to remain ahead of aggressive competitors.

This discussion of the limitations of financial analysis methods is not intended to discourage their use. They are an essential part of understanding any business plan or operation, and methods of financial analysis and management accounting do evolve to respond to changing conditions. One example is the emergence of an "options" theory of R&D investment (options pricing theory) that explicitly treats research and development expenditures as financial options. By paying now to preserve a future opportunity, this technique deals with the problem of uncertainty in R&D and with the cost of not acting. More context-specific techniques must, however, complement financial considerations—techniques that are sensitive to the key success factors of particular commercialization efforts. In the realm of management accounting there is a growing awareness of the need to collect and use financial and operational information that is better designed to aid decision making.[3]

Thus, the search that each manager must undertake is for a broad-based set of tools, both formal and intuitive, that measure the fundamental aspects of the business. This tool kit should consist of methods for filtering useful business information out of the jumble of information about operations, competitors, market growth, sales performance, and, particularly, technological opportunities.

Imagination is the only limit to the number of possible performance indicators, but there are only a few underlying purposes for measuring performance: (a) to understand better the markets for existing or new products or services, (b) to predict internal performance or measure actual performance against plans or predictions, (c) to compare a company's performance to that of others carrying out similar functions, (d) to forecast the development of technology, (e) to consider the strengths and weaknesses of an operation in relation to the market or technological environment, and (f) to build the expectation of improvement. Each of these purposes is important at different times in the life of a company commercializing new products and services.

EVALUATING A COMPANY'S PERFORMANCE
IN NEW PRODUCT COMMERCIALIZATION

Evaluation of commercialization performance is difficult and may rely on such gross measures as the structure of R&D activity in a firm, the historical performance of an important competitor in launching new products, or a "product portfolio" comparison that matches the maturity of a company's products against the maturity of a competitor's products.

The literature is filled with methods of analyzing business product portfolios—usually on two-dimensional grids comparing measures of growth potential and business return. These are helpful for establishing business strategy. Other portfolio measurements, based on the time for a product, process, or service to reach the market, are sensitive to company commercialization performance.

Two types of portfolio measurements are now commonly used and can be of considerable value. First, a company can simply display its own sales by year of product introduction as shown in Figure 3–2. Second, the same type of data displayed for competitors can dramatically illustrate the commercialization (new product introduction) performance of each marketplace competitor. Both allow consideration of whether a firm is performing adequately in new products or services. Such data are useful, of course, only if care is taken to distinguish truly new products from those new product introductions that reflect only cosmetic changes.

Product maturity information is especially valuable when combined with internal company information on production process efficiency and flexibility. Product development cycle time, design changeover time, parts inventory level, work-in-process level, capital utilization, and speed with which new designs are produced can give managers a feel for their company's commercialization capabilities. Services production (transportation, communications, engineering design, and finance, for example) is more diverse than manufactur-

Figure 3–2 Hewlett-Packard Product Orders, by Year Introduced

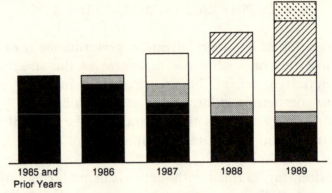

1985 and Prior Years	1986	1987	1988	1989

Each bar indicates the year's total product orders; the top section of each bar shows orders for products introduced in that year. More than half of 1989's orders were for products introduced in the past three years.

SOURCE: Hewlett-Packard Annual Report, 1989, p. 2

ing. It is often harder to measure both inputs and outputs for comparison in these cases, but it can be done.

UNDERSTANDING TECHNOLOGICAL COMPETENCE OF EXISTING BUSINESSES

Assessment of the fit of a company's technological competence with planned product or service development is critical. A company's technological competence is more than simply the patents and licenses it controls. While technology in the narrowest sense can be characterized as stand-alone, explicit knowledge that is closely held and easily contained, technological competence is different. "Core" competence is often embodied in systems and relies on tacit know-how resident within the personnel, routines, and practices of a firm. As such it is difficult to uproot or unbundle. An example is Honda's core competence with engines, which allowed the company to participate effectively in markets for cars, lawn mowers, motorcycles, garden tractors, chain saws, and generators.

New business development experiences contain many examples of otherwise successful companies that, in spite of being early to develop a technology, were unable to convert their leadership into market success. Instead, other, later entrants managed to capitalize on the opportunity.

It was 1973 when researchers at Xerox's Palo Alto Research Center (PARC) completed work on Alto, the first computer to be designed and built for dedicated use by one person. The system incorporated a list of "firsts." It had the first graphics-oriented monitor, the first hand-held "mouse" input device, the first word processing program for nonexpert users, the first local area communications network, the first object-oriented programming language, the first laser printer. All of this before the appearance of the Apple II or IBM's attempts to be a force in the personal computer market. Why is Xerox's Alto not a household word today? A number of factors coalesced to deter Xerox from being a major player in the personal computer market. Most particularly, Xerox had lost its vision of the future.

By 1979 Xerox was no longer the resilient company it once had been due to outside influences—fierce competition, government antagonism, economic recession. Internal forces, however, played an even bigger role in the company's loss of confidence. Xerox traditionally followed a deliberate, albeit expensive, plan for marketing technology. It had spent hundreds of millions of dollars over several years to develop copiers before bringing them to market. But personal computing presented a different problem. It was a problem of how customers would react to the technology—how people would respond to computers they could program and use themselves. To answer these questions, Xerox would have to spend $10 million, maybe $25 million. But the company chose not to spend this relatively modest amount, indicating either that the sum was not impressive enough to Xerox or that the company believed it had nothing to learn from potential *customers. In either case, what this says is that Xerox could not cope with a technology as different from copiers as digital computers.*

To make the situation worse, Xerox's upper management surrendered its decision-making role in introducing new technology. Joe Wilson, Xerox CEO during the era of copier development, made the decisions about the Model A Copier that failed and the 914 Copier that succeeded. Peter McColough, who had funded PARC, deliberately took no part in the underlying management structure that for various reasons worked to keep advances a secret from those who would buy. This happened because senior management was a cadre that placed primary emphasis on finance and control. This philosophy permitted tackling only what was already accepted with technology that was already developed. Thus, they would exploit leadership in a market only when that leadership already existed. This problem was exacerbated by Xerox's new unwillingness to learn. By bringing the copier to market, Joe Wilson and his colleagues learned about their mistakes and used this knowledge to build better copiers. By keeping Alto a secret, Wilson's successors ensured there was no experience, no learning, no advance.[4]

There are many reasons that companies fail to commercialize technologies effectively. Failure to exploit a particular opportunity rarely has a single cause. Poor planning, lack of a champion, underfunding, failure to understand what has to be done to succeed, and failures of individuals to execute their responsibilities all figure in flubbed opportunities. Often, however, it appears that companies simply are unable to cope with technological opportunities that require them to adopt new production methods, face new competitors, or cultivate customers in different ways.

When this happens to an individual, we say that he or she is trying to do a task for which he is not competent. Just like individuals, organizations have areas of competence and of incompetence. Such areas can include technical capability, knowledge of customer needs and desires, and mastery of marketing channels or of manufacturing processes. Competence of an organization goes beyond formal skills required to practice an activity. It is embedded in almost a visceral fashion in the way the firm does business; it embodies the desires and commitments of the group as a whole. Competence is reflected in the technical skills of the staff, the thinking patterns of the management, the values embraced throughout the company, and organizational experiences.

The Pulitzer-prize-winning business historian Alfred D. Chandler describes organizational capabilities as the determinant of competitive performance for the most successful industrial enterprises of the last century:

> At the core of this dynamic were the organizational capabilities of the enterprise as a unified whole. These organizational capabilities were the collective physical facilities and human skills as they were organized within the enterprise. They included the physical facilities in each of many operating units—the factories, office, laboratories—and the skills of employees working in such units. But only if these facilities and skills were carefully coordinated and integrated could the enterprise achieve the economies of scale and scope that were needed to compete in national and international markets and to continue to grow.[5]

Chandler goes on to attribute most of the responsibility for creating organizational capability to active management of the industrial enterprise. In his analysis, this capability is a cascade that begins at the top of the organization, but one that depends on committed and capable management right down to the operating level.

Understanding a company's organizational capabilities— its strengths and weaknesses—and working to maintain and develop those competencies is perhaps the crucial management skill.[6] However, assessing the competence of a company—and understanding areas of incompetence as well—is mostly an art. Although some analytical tools apply, two people can look at the same organization and see quite different underlying strengths. Explicit consideration of core capabilities is, however, an exercise well worth performing, as the introspection needed to characterize the core competencies of an organization can suggest areas of future development that build on existing strengths, or areas of business development that can strengthen and extend present skills to allow entry into new markets. Assessment of core competencies can also provide the basis for understanding what part of the commercialization process can be best carried out within the company, and what must be addressed through outside contract resources, alliances with other firms, or strategic acquisitions.

EVALUATING NEW PRODUCTS, PROCESSES, AND SERVICE OPPORTUNITIES

One aspect of measuring and managing a company's new product commercialization performance is building the ability to evaluate the promise of new technologies and the products or services based on new technologies when development is still in the laboratory stage. 3M has developed and uses a system of technical audits to do such assessments.

Since 1963, 3M has performed "technical audits" of all major 3M laboratory programs. Every two to three years, major research programs are assessed, the overall health of laboratories is evaluated, and recommendations on product programs, technology areas, and laboratory issues are provided to management. Programs evaluated include (1) major new product programs (those on which significant investments are being made and/or those projected to have the largest sales impact), (2) technology building efforts, (3) process development and cost-savings programs, and (4) product maintenance work (such as incremental product improvements).
    Programs are rated on:

Technical Factors

- *Overall technology strength (breadth, patentability, competitiveness)*
- *Personnel (numbers, skills)*
- *Competitive factors (knowledge of competition, 3M product performance)*
- *Remaining R&D investment (in relation to time to complete the program)*
- *Manufacturing implementation (feasibility, cost, protectability)*
- *Probability of technical success*

Business Factors

- *Financial potential (sales, profits)*
- *3M competitive position (marketing channels, product value)*
- *Probability of marketing success*

Overall Factors

- *Organization and planning (strategy, focus, clarity of goals)*
- *Staffing (numbers, skills)*
- *Program balance (between maintenance of existing products and work on new products)*
- *Coordination and interaction (with marketing, manufacturing, other 3M labs)*

The auditors provide both numerical ratings and essay comments in each of the areas. Using those ratings, the planning staff calculates a probability of technical success and a probability of marketing success. Working with a rich data base containing nearly 25 years of information, the planning department has spent considerable time studying auditors' ratings in relation to the actual results of 3M's product programs. It has been found that the overall probability of program success, obtained by multiplying the probability of technical success by the probability of marketing success, correctly predicts a program's outcome a high percentage of the time.

Ongoing studies of programs on related new products have also shown that, in addition to probability of success and sales, the following factors have a statistically significant effect on R&D success or failure in work on related products:

- *Competitive position of 3M business unit developing the product*
- *3M product performance in relation to the competition*
- *Degree to which the technology is related to 3M's existing technical base*
- *Degree to which the market is related to 3M's existing business base*

In work on unrelated new products, the uniqueness or "newness to the world" of the product being developed and the competitive position (in the closest industry) of the 3M business unit developing the product have proven to be important determinants of success.[7]

The technical audits are a mechanism by which 3M management obtains a consistent overview of the company's diverse R&D activities. The audits assess 3M's attention to business maintenance, its potential for growth from related or unrelated new products, and the health of its technologies.

Successful products and services, whether they emerge from new technologies or from the market's pull on existing technologies, reflect customer desires for quality, function, and price. Well-managed ongoing operations maintain constant feedback between customers' demands and product improvement efforts.

The first, and often primary, challenge in planning the development of innovative technology-based products or services is getting a deep understanding of the potential market. Sometimes, the market for a new technology is clear, as illustrated by Figure 3–3, which shows the growth in transatlantic telecommunications messages—actual and estimated—over a period of 40 years. With such sustained growth, the market for a technologically new product was almost certain, but the specific challenge was to identify the correct technology—a fiber-optic transatlantic cable or satellite communication—and bring it to market. The major challenge with regard to the transatlantic fiber-optic cable that AT&T completed in 1988 was to develop a new technology and prove 25-year reliability in time to meet market demand. Many other factors affect the ability of a company like AT&T to share in that market. Often in commercializing new products or services, however, the challenge is in designing nonexistent products for nonexistent markets—determining "what the customer wants" without the benefit of any market experience with the product or service.

Traditional market research often fails when assessing new products or services. There is often no prior market experience, and customer preferences cannot be measured if they do not yet exist. New products and services can be bad

Figure 3–3 Actual and Forecast Transatlantic Messages

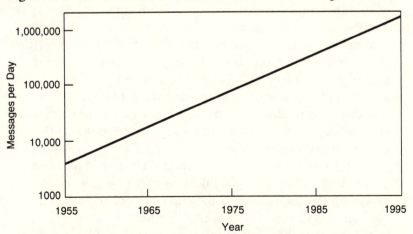

SOURCE: William Macurdy, former vice president for transmission systems, AT&T Bell Laboratories, in remarks presented during National Academy of Engineering Workshop on Profiting from Innovation, Woods Hole, Mass., August 1988.

ideas or great ideas, but they are uniformly unfamiliar to customers. In such cases it is important to have the vision to look through current consumers to the market that will exist. In new product or service development, an internally generated vision of the market success factors must be developed. Such market vision characterizes the ability to make a product out of a discovery, as was the case for E-A-R®.

The objectives of Cabot's purchase of National Research Corporation (NRC) in the early seventies were to secure a strong cadre of research professionals, most of whom were chemical and metallurgical engineers by training, and a portfolio of patents focused on electronics applications of silicon carbide in both bulk and film form. At the initial R&D review of the NRC work, I discovered a small materials effort aimed at vibration and noise control in industrial environments. Under Norton ownership, NRC had patented a variety of polymeric materials that they had learned to make and use as energy absorbers. One of these was a sheet vinyl that had been modified by chemical additives so that pound for pound it was the best known polymeric energy absorber. The material was demonstrated to me as a blue ball (golf ball sized), which when thrown on a concrete floor didn't bounce up—it just hit the floor and stayed there.

Nobody had any suggestions as to what we might do with the material other than use it to absorb vibration under motors or reduce aggravating clanging of metal parts in foundry and steel mill operations. At my prodding over the next six months, NRC modified the material in a variety of ways including making it in foam and padding form. But still there were no applications.

When I was shown the foam version, we used it as a coaster for hot coffee cups. Everyone noticed that when the cup was picked up the impression of the cup's bottom remained behind only to vanish slowly over about one minute's time. In thinking about that, one of the NRC scientists, Ross Gardner, realized that the combined properties of (1) high-energy absorption, (2) slow recovery after deformation, and (3) foam were the prescription for an ideal earplug. It took less than a year to learn how to make E-A-R® plugs—to test them adequately—to build a pilot plant—to launch the sales effort—and, most remarkably, to get into the black.

Today, E-A-R® dominates the hearing protection market in every country in the world.[8]

The value of a firm vision of new product and service development cannot be overestimated. While such concepts are often incorrect in their specifics, they provide the focus necessary to move forward. In this context, there is no substitute for a manager or technical professional committed to making a new technology work in commercial applications of the future. This requires early and frequent interaction with the marketplace. In other cases, markets have to be created over time. Many classic examples of this type of challenge come from materials innovations as inventors look for applications that are not obvious either to producers of the materials or to users unfamiliar with their properties. The market for new materials often depends on many other developments and, hence, often develops slowly.

Depending on how dramatic a technological or market change is envisioned, classical market research methods for new products and services may or may not be useful. Most market research methods rely on marketplace tests of prototype products and some combination of focus groups or aggressively interactive discussion (not merely a survey) with customers or potential customers. Intensive interaction is necessary to overcome customer uncertainty about products and services that do not exist, a kind of exploration of potential with both producers and consumers represented.[9]

Forcefully executed and evaluated marketplace tests serve the same purpose but give body to the more abstract discussions. An existing customer base can be a crucial asset in carrying out such tests. The Du Pont Company's experience with its fibers business—a business with great successes such as Tyvek® and Kevlar® but also some significant failures—is typical:

> Testing the market early is the only way to figure out if you have a viable product. You'll learn not only whether a need exists for the product but also the value of the product. One way to get at this issue is to ask what your product does better than any other available product. If the answer is "nothing," you may not have a viable product. It is very important to do this before finalizing the design of a full-scale commercial production facility.
>
> We always seem to get a few surprises at this stage—some good, some bad. The market is never, in real life, quite like we imagined it to be from inside our corporate walls. While this is important for all new products, it is particularly important for new products that are toward the "technology driven" end of the spectrum. I could cite countless examples of where our internal product development research was close to the mark on defining the value and potential of a new product concept, but still off the mark. The product either had to be modified or the marketing strategy adjusted before the product became a success. Of course, in a few cases we have missed the mark entirely. Here, I know of no substitute for close and continual marketplace interaction by the product development and marketing people. You must test and adjust, test and adjust, and then do it several more times to successfully bring a new form of matter to commercialization. I also emphasize that the research people themselves must be directly involved in interacting with the marketplace. They cannot depend on another person's interpretation of the results. The people responsible for developing the product must see the problems the customer has with it first hand.[10]

Products and services based on both technology-driven and market-driven opportunities are, for most companies, decisions made at the margin: "Shall we begin this effort in earnest?" As such, decisions are particularly amenable to break-even analyses and tracking—a marginal analysis that collects costs and revenues over time.

TRACKING PROJECT PROGRESS

In the course of a project, it is easy to lose sight of the final objective—to introduce a profitable product into the market or process to manufacturing. Changes in project direction, unexpected events during development and manufacturing implementation, changes in market expectations, or simply infatuation with the technology can distract senior managers from this critical goal.

The manager, faced with periodically reviewing a portfolio of commercialization efforts, must have decision-making tools to guide his attention to problem areas. They should be simple to apply and easy to understand, and they should show progress, incorporate important management decision factors, apply throughout the life of the project, and provide an early indication of changes in the project status. It is important that such tools focus on the end objective of the project—commercialization success—and not become bogged down in details of current tasks.

A manager has many tools available to track project progress against milestones set forth in project plans. Both Pert and Gantt chart tracking methods are widely used, and they are valuable methods for considering progress against a predetermined detailed schedule.

Two additional techniques can add important extra dimensions to project progress assessments. The first is a checklist of the activities and decision points as a development project progresses. The second is time-to-break-even analysis, a method of tracking total project return all the way through the marketing stage.

STAGES OF DEVELOPMENT

Some major decision points in commercialization of products and processes based on new technologies are more obvious than others. At such points, decisions to proceed with commercialization often entail commitment to significantly greater investment.

While there is tremendous variation in the character of commercialization projects, most projects proceed by stages from concept to fielded products. The decision to complete each stage and move on to the next represents renewed and increased commitment. Typically the cost of each stage is five to ten times higher than that of its predecessor. It is important, therefore, to understand the objective of each stage and questions that must be answered before completion of that stage of activity. Commercialization management skills include understanding the nature of project progression and knowing what issues must be addressed before making the commitment to continue to the next stage.

The National Society of Professional Engineers, in cooperation with the National Institute of Standards and Technology, has characterized the various stages in the realization of a new product, process, or service.[11] Each stage has characteristic activities building to a decision point where answers to typical questions must be determined. These six stages are Concept, Technical Feasibility, Development, Commercial Validation and Production Preparation, Full-Scale Production, and Product Support.

Although these stages are presented here in "linear" order, from concept to production and product support, specific projects may loop through several stages as iterations of design and production technology evolve. This is particularly true in product- and process-improvement commercialization. The stages are described, as formulated by a task group of the National Society of Professional Engineers,[12] to show how information about a product or service and its market builds over time as a company pursues a commercialization project.

During the *Concept* stage, the new product, process, or service concept is proven scientifically valid and its applicability shown through analysis or a test-of-principle model.

Typical Activities

- Articulate the concept
- Confirm critical assumptions
- Identify critical manufacturing barriers
- Survey the state of the art

Information Developed

- Concept description
- Target specifications, goals
- Results of tests
- Identification of barriers to development, manufacturing, marketing
- How the concept "fits" into a marketable product

The objective of the *Technical Feasibility* stage is to confirm the target performance of a product, process, or service through experimentation or analysis and to understand the technical and economic obstacles that must be overcome.

Typical Activities

- Test for technical feasibility
- Examine operational requirements
- Identify potential safety or environmental hazards
- Assess production feasibility

Information Developed

- Performance based on bench model
- Preliminary product or process design
- Preliminary development plans, including cost, marketing, safety and environmental concerns, and manufacturing
- Plans for the next stage, including cost and time schedule

The *Development* stage focuses on improvements in material, design, and processes and on confirmation of performance by constructing and testing engineering prototypes and pilot processes.

Typical Activities	*Information Developed*
• Identify critical materials, and develop components and process steps • Test critical materials, components, and process steps • Design and fabricate a prototype or pilot process • Optimize the product through design iterations • Conduct final performance tests	• Proof of performance by prototype or pilot process • Description of manufacturing methods and materials • Description of safety and environmental issues • Proof of expected reliability • Refined marketing strategy given cost and manufacturing estimates

The *Commercial Validation and Production Preparation* stage is the period for preparing a product or process for introduction into the factory or marketplace. A comprehensive plan for commercial introduction should result.

Typical Activities	*Information Developed*
• Complete preproduction prototype • Determine the preproduction process • Select manufacturing procedures and equipment • Demonstrate effectiveness of the design, process, production tools and technology, materials and components, and market acceptance • Establish vendor base • Design a field support system	• Performance data based on manufacturable prototype or preproduction process • Maintainability and reliability data • Manufacturing data • Materials and components lists • Spare parts plans • Installation and operational cost data • Updated safety and environmental data • Test market characteristics and data • Warranty and service plans • Confirmation of manufacturing time and cost projections

Information Developed

- Assurance of installation within time and cost constraints
- Verification of operability under full-scale production
- Compliance with health, safety, and environmental standards
- Verification of performance producibility

The *Full-Scale Production* stage is the period for producing the product, process, or service consistent with market demand. This stage includes minor improvements and persists as long as manufacturing continues.

Typical Activities

Initially:
- Complete commercial designs
- Detail the manufacturing process
- Complete quality control procedures at all levels of procurement and production
- Complete the distribution
- Construct and equip manufacturing facilities
- Trial run production

Ongoing:
- Make evolutionary improvement in production products and processes
- Reenter earlier stages for extensive modifications

Information Developed

- Production drawings and schematics
- Manufacturing flow charts
- Documentation of production operations
- Quality control and reliability standards
- Final market acceptance testing
- Identification of distribution and customer assistance plans
- Assessment of production process and product activities, emphasizing possible engineering improvement

The goal of the *Product Support* stage is to maintain the maximum value of the product or process through improvements and customer support.

Typical Activities

- Issue on-site instructions and updates for safe and effective use of the product or process
- Prepare, distribute, and encourage use of instruction manuals
- Design, produce, and distribute "consumables" used with the product or process
- Design and introduce timely improvements in materials, components, systems, and software
- Produce and distribute spare parts
- Provide warranty services
- Devise and introduce new applications
- Identify new product spin-offs and major changes that require return to earlier stages
- Distribute alerts and take remedial actions for unplanned product deficiencies or changing safety and environmental standards

Activities and information characteristics of each stage may vary somewhat in specific industries, but the intent remains the same—to complete stage activities and produce information sufficient to decide whether to go on to the next stage.

TIME-TO-BREAK-EVEN ANALYSIS

Time-to-break-even analysis is a simple management tool that can be used throughout the course of execution of a commercialization project. It is not a useful tool to select between alternative projects at the initial decision-making time. Instead, it is a means of tracking performance of a commercialization project already under way. Time-to-break-even analysis summarizes experience, current outlook, and the ultimate goal in a simple, easy-to-work with format. It provides more useful information than conventional indicators, such as budget to actual expense comparisons. Time-to-break-even analysis embodies many factors that affect project progress to date and forecast completion and market acceptance.

Simply put, the time-to-break-even graph[13] is the net investment plotted over the life of the project. Figure 3–4 shows a typical time-to-break-even analysis. The dotted lines show cumulative expense incurred and income generated (either from additional sales or cost savings). The time-to-break-even curve (the solid line) is simply the sum of the expense and income curves. Early in the life of a project, there are no sales (or savings); development and manufacturing initiation expenses are incurred. After product introduction or process manufacturing start-up, marginal income or savings accumulate as the start-up costs drop. The time to break-even is when the net investment reaches zero.

The time-to-break-even curve is a simple, yet valuable,

Figure 3–4 Time-to-Break-Even Curve Shows When Net Investment in a Product Reaches Zero

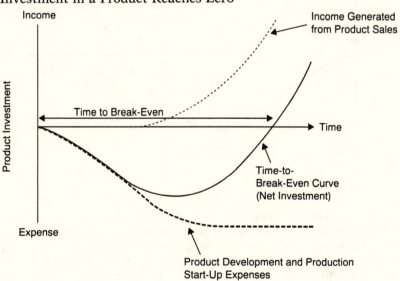

project management tool. It incorporates many financial concerns of the company: the cash flow required for a development project, the time required to repay the investment, and market return. In this respect, the time-to-break-even curve is a valuable planning tool at the outset of the effort to anticipate the course the project will take. A family of time-to-break-even curves can illustrate the range of assumptions made during the planning process to estimate the effect of changes in schedule, cost, and market acceptance.

Time-to-break-even analysis is also valuable when assessing the progress of a project under way. Figure 3–5 shows the time-to-break-even analysis under different project progress scenarios. With elapsed project history and latest estimates

Figure 3–5 Time-to-Break-Even Curves as a Project-Tracking Tool

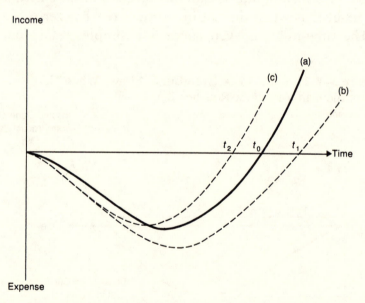

(a) Initial planning nominal curve. (b) Part way into the project, expenses are greater than planned and forecast time to break-even has slipped out (t_0 to t_1). This indicates possible project problems that require more detailed examination of the project plan and activity. (c) Corrections made in the project activity have improved expense and break-even time. This project is now less likely to be a problem.

of project completion and market updates, the progress of the effort toward meeting its goal becomes clear. If the nominal time to break-even is within the initial planned range, or is moving earlier as commercialization approaches, the project is likely to be in good shape.

An increasing time to break-even is an early warning of trouble. If the time to break-even is moving beyond the initial planning assumptions, it is time to reassess the effort—its progress, the changing market scenario, or the investment required. Such an early warning signal is crucial; it allows the manager to take action while the problems are small, and more likely to be solvable, rather than to wait until real trouble develops.

Time-to-break-even analysis is a simple tool—it is an elementary rule of thumb that enables managers quickly to size up project status. Such rules are only cursory examinations, however, and are not a replacement for a more detailed understanding of the project. The tool is only as valid as the realism of the assumptions that go into its calculation.

EVALUATING PRODUCT- AND PROCESS-IMPROVEMENT OPPORTUNITIES

Opportunities for product- and process-improvement commercialization are ubiquitous. In any business there are always opportunities to improve existing products, processes, and services, and much of this activity is technological in nature. Furthermore, technological options are often unclear at the beginning of a project intended to revive or improve a product or service. Will designs based on idea A or idea B be easier to manufacture, maintain, and sell? What is the trade-off between cost and function in the customer's mind, and how does that affect the choice of technological approach? Is it time to reinvest in an older technology or to pursue a less certain new technology?

In most product- and process-improvement efforts, technological change is evolutionary, and the pace of development can be forecast, as shown by the lightwave systems example in Figure 3–6. In other cases, forecasting may be a matter of understanding product life cycles. Figures 3–7 and 3–8 show the pattern of sales of successive generations of a technological product. A variety of models and approaches are useful and no comprehensive review is given here. The diversity and changing nature of production processes—as well as the number of options for improvement in everything from procurement to design, from inventory control to engineering productivity, or from changeover times to field service—makes it impossible to set uniform evaluation procedures. Instead, this section picks just a few common techniques of analysis of production matters of this kind. It attempts to show how the constant and persistent application of quantitative or structured qualitative analysis of these types of issues can offer valuable insights to managers at several levels of the organization.

BENCHMARKING

Direct comparison of performance (called benchmarking) between a company and others with similar operations can

Figure 3–6 Lightwave Technology Capacity–Distance Achievements, 1975–1990

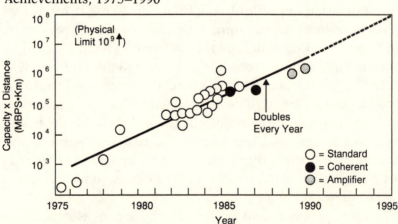

SOURCE: AT&T Bell Laboratories.

Figure 3–7 DRAM Product Life Cycles (by Density over Time)

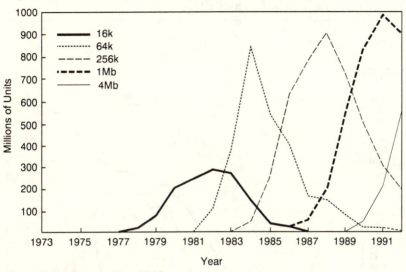

SOURCE: *Dataquest*, May 1988.

be invaluable. The comparisons may be with competitors or others who are the best in specific business activities, such as warehousing or field service. Comparisons can take the following forms:

1. Product comparisons (features, age, design for manufacturability, cost, reliability, quality)
2. Service comparisons (quality, response times, on-time delivery record, price, features)
3. Operational comparisons (warehousing, manufacturing changeover times, direct and indirect labor usage)

Such information can be a powerful motivator for management; a sound understanding of exactly where and how others do better gives a company clear and achievable improvement targets. Xerox Corporation had such a motivating experience in the early 1980s.

In the late sixties and seventies Xerox was a copier company and only a copier company. Since Xerox invented the art the company was capitalizing on it—Xerox was the only copier

Figure 3–8. Life Cycle Curves Show Past Product History in Order to Project New Product's Life

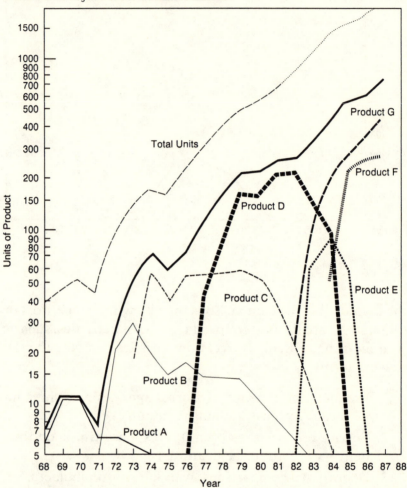

SOURCE: C. H. Willyard and C. W. McClees, "Motorola's Technology Road-map Process," *Research Management*, September–October 1987, p. 15. Copyright© 1987 Motorola, Inc. Reprinted with permission.

company in the world and making money hand over fist. By the mid-seventies Xerox was buying and selling computer companies and managed to start competing with IBM and AT&T simultaneously. It is well-chronicled that this effort cost Xerox hundreds of millions of dollars. During that period of time Xerox's market share in copiers went from more than 90 percent (in the early 1970s) to about 20 percent (in the late 1970s).

In 1979 one manager in the corporation finally figured out that this was a problem and sent a team of engineers to Japan to find out what they were doing that was different from our practices. The team came back with the following sobering information. The Japanese manufacturers that were competing with Xerox were making the product at half of Xerox's manufacturing cost. The quality of their parts was a factor of 30 better than Xerox's, their development schedules were roughly half and the size of the development teams was roughly half—some of us started to wonder if we shouldn't look around for some other business. Of course, the team returns from Japan and delivers its findings and the first thing that happens is that no one believes it. In fact, as it turned out, it was not quite right—the situation was worse than the numbers led one to believe. It was a real attention getter. In a very short time after the team returned the senior management of Xerox—the top 15 senior officers of the corporation—went about learning about quality.[14]

Product and service comparisons involve both customer perceptions—factors that affect the purchase decision—and internal business activities. In manufactured products, such things as parts count, number of types of fasteners, ease of assembly, and interchangeability of components within a product line are clues about a competitor's product design and production process. They also imply a great deal about product quality. This kind of detail is raw material for thinking about better design for manufacturability. In services, features like reliability, availability, service performance, and quality are crucial; they are windows on a competitor's production process.

All too often, the basis of expectations for business improvement is extrapolation of internal company experience. In those industries where employees move frequently between competing companies, this experience base might be expanded to include an industry-wide perspective. Yet, neither of these can raise company expectations to the highest realistic level. The task of identifying company goals must be

expanded to look deliberately beyond company experience—
even beyond the experience of an entire industry—to gain an
appreciation for best performance possibilities.

"Best-in-class" companies achieve top performance for a
given function within an enterprise, measured against the
world's best firms. Understanding best-in-class performance
is critical to understanding how and where to push for improvement.

The search for best-in-class examples must be a broad one.
It requires hard work, knowledge, humility, and exceptional
insight into practices of a wide range of companies. For a
given company function, the best-in-class company may not
be a competitor. In one instance, a major office equipment
manufacturer seeking to set performance goals for its spare
parts warehousing operation found the best example of efficient, responsive, cost-effective warehousing was a retail,
mail-order, sporting goods company. The search for best-in-
class examples must extend across the widest possible industry base to find the most aggressive realistic goals and
hints on how to attain them.

The benchmarking process (see Figure 3–9) compares existing company performance with that of the best-of-class
performer. When done persistently for each company function, management can develop a real-time feel for where
improvements are possible and realistic expectations for
how much improvement is possible.

Benchmarking generally does not set hard goals for how
much progress is possible. There is always room for new
ideas that lead to yet better performance. It provides a source
of ideas for improvement expectations that goes beyond
internal experience. It is important to note that effective
benchmarking involves more than analyzing the competition.[15]

ASSESSING LEARNING

The basis of product- and process-improvement commercialization efforts is the drive for continuous improve-

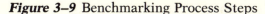

Figure 3–9 Benchmarking Process Steps

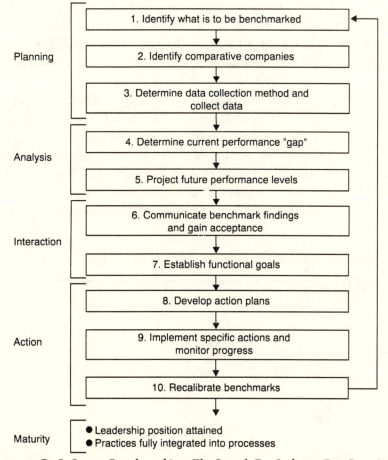

SOURCE: R. C. Camp, *Benchmarking: The Search For Industry Best Practices that Lead to Superior Performance* (Milwaukee, Wisc.: ASQC Quality Press, 1989), p. 259. Reprinted with the permission of ASQC.

ment. Improvement must be driven—it does not happen by itself. Useful tools for managing product- and process-improvement activities must focus on expectation of improvement and its pace.

Learning curves (also called experience curves or progress functions) are a means of assessing rate of improvement in an ongoing production and design environment. Learning-curve analysis developed from the observation that experience gained in production activities shows up in more efficient production and improved product designs. There is a vast literature on the application and misapplication of learning curves, most of which illustrates the same basic and important point: learning in a company goes on throughout the production life of the product. The effects of experience can be best seen when unit costs and inputs such as labor hours per unit produced are plotted against accumulated manufacturing volume on a logarithmic graph.[16]

Figure 3–10 shows a plot of average labor hours per unit against cumulative number of units produced. Figure 3–11 shows average selling price and average cost of a product against cumulative production. Note that despite short-term

Figure 3–10 Cumulative Man-hours per Unit Curve

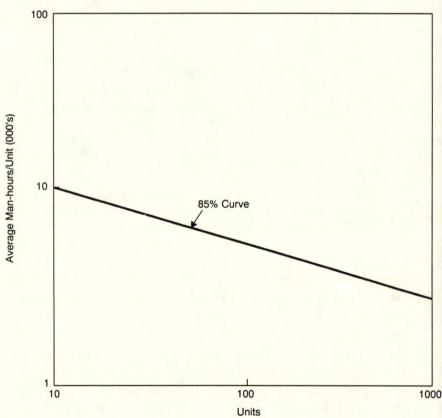

Figure 3–11 Experience Curve Predicts Future Costs and Prices from Historical Data (Costs are in constant 1972 dollars)

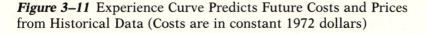

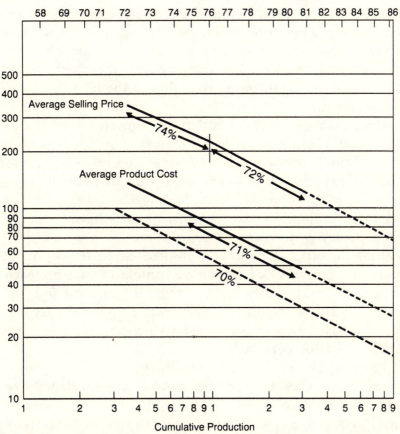

Cumulative Production

SOURCE: C. H. Willyard and C. W. McClees, "Motorola's Technology Road-map Process," *Research Management*, September–October 1987, p. 16. Copyright © 1987 Motorola, Inc. Reprinted with permission.

fluctuations, the long-term trend approximates a straight line (on a log-log plot). The slope of the line is the drop in cost for each doubling of accumulated volume (the total number of units produced since the start of the production activity). Industries tend to have characteristic slopes; for many parts of the electronics business, production costs tend to decrease by 30 percent for each doubling of accumulated production volume—a slope of 70 percent.

The learning phenomenon is the result of many small, discrete events, the effects of which accumulate to produce the improvement trend. In its detail, the learning curve is really a series of steps, each an individual improvement event. The trend line is a measure of incremental "learning" progress in an ongoing design and production activity. Learning curves cannot, however, anticipate the impact of major shifts in technology or organization that change the basic nature of the enterprise.

Once managements noted that learning curves characterized long-term performance in diverse industries, expectation of the learning process became a useful management tool for expectation of future improvements. For the manager, learning curves do more than forecast; they provide a basis for evaluating past and anticipated rates of progress for industry performance. They also provide a basis for impelling the organization to put in place activities to provide future progress. Since learning is a cumulative effect, a learning curve consistently steeper than the general industry slope is likely to result in a more competitive product line. One that is not up to the industry rate suggests a firm less likely to be competitive.

Learning curves are tools to be used in planning a project to estimate whether projected results are sufficient to remain competitive. The same tool is also useful to assess the general improvement in performance of an ongoing activity. It should serve to stimulate actions needed to cause improvements before competitiveness starts to slip.

The learning curve phenomenon may not be limited to production costs. In some instances this tool has proven to be a useful indicator of progress in other product and process attributes: quality levels, size and weight of portable products, energy consumption, scrap production, manufacturing cycle time, and operating speed. The formulation of learning-curve projections in these noncost areas is product dependent and has not been carefully documented.

Learning-curve analysis provides a simple overview of progress toward product and process improvement. It builds the sense of expectation of continuous improvement needed to keep pushing technological developments that form the basis for future competitive leadership. In addition, it indicates the extent of improvement likely to be needed in the future to develop or retain leadership.

TECHNOLOGY ROADMAPS

Expectational tools, such as learning curves, give important insight into attainable product- and process-development goals. Managers must then determine specific supporting technology developments that must be accomplished to reach the overall objective. The technology roadmap is one example of a working-level management tool that aids identification and development of supporting technologies.

The technology roadmap is a technology development scenario consistent with changing product and production needs. In essence, the roadmap method is an orderly process for devising a picture of future technology. The roadmap is a projection of major technological elements of product design and manufacturing over time. The period covered by the technology roadmap should encompass the time needed to develop or adapt technologies to use. Companies that plan their other business operations 5 years out may find it necessary to adopt 10-year technology roadmaps so that appropriate technology can be ready for timely application.

The technology roadmap development process requires as complete an understanding of competitive behavior, product life, and production needs as possible. The roadmap combines information from many other management tools discussed earlier in a consistent planning scenario. Preparation for roadmap formulation includes collection of data on product life cycles, learning curves, competitive analysis, and any other indicators of product, market, and manufacturing activities.[17]

The process begins with development of product market outlooks and competitive and technological outlooks. Because roadmap time frames tend to extend well beyond conventional business planning horizons, product planning and marketing personnel will find it necessary to project well beyond current product plans. The product scenario must be visionary and aggressive, but reflect feasible customer needs. It must identify the vision of the product future, including product features, performance attributes, likely markets, and selling prices.

Design and manufacturing personnel are then asked to critique the marketing vision and to figure out what technological attributes they must have to produce the forecast products. Again, since the roadmap looks farther into the future than many other company planning processes, both design and production engineers must brainstorm to identify or invent technical solutions to future product and manufacturing problems. Participants in this part of the process, in considering the most distant product horizon, must look beyond current technology and methods to develop insight.

The results of the technology roadmap planning process, which may require several iterations to converge on a satisfactory vision, can be thought of as a cube, as Figure 3–12 shows. One dimension is product characteristics, one is product design technology, and one is production technology. Each dimension relates to the other two so that the roadmap is internally consistent. In practice the roadmap document consists of three charts showing three aspects of technology development—one highlighting the product and its technology, the second manufacturing process technologies, and the third general support requirements, such as computer-aided design tools, and field support needs. Each chart presents time lines for each major technology element and its required evolution to support the rest of the plan. Figure 3–13 shows a typical product chart.

Support for all developments required to make a comprehensive technology roadmap a reality can be beyond the ability of any single company. Reduction of the roadmap scenario to a sensible plan of action requires several additional steps. First, identify design, process, and support tech-

Figure 3–12 The Roadmap Planning Process Is
Three-Dimensional

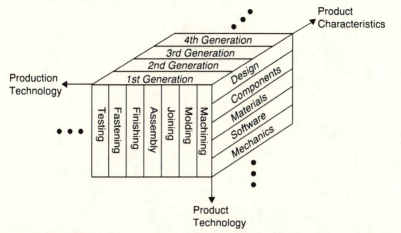

Visions of product characteristics, product technology and production
technology must all fit together to form a comprehensive development
scenario. In a sense, the finished plan is a "cube" consisting of
individual product, product technology, and production technology
elements.

nology developments that are common to several product
lines. Identify the earliest need for the development, and
plan for that. The rest will follow automatically. Second,
look for those elements that represent distinctive competitive advantages that may be protected by patents or trade
secrets. Third, identify those elements that are likely to be
available outside the company; deciding whether to make or
buy these elements is important in executing technology
roadmap plans. David Teece's work[18] on capturing value
from technological innovations is particularly useful in addressing these decisions.

The result of this filtering process should be a much
smaller group of technical challenges, a group of "keystone"
technologies—those that will provide the base for future
competitive advantage. The keystone technologies form the
core of the technology development strategy for the firm.

The emphasis in the technology roadmap process must be
on thinking out future options. Although the roadmap is a

Figure 3–13 Hypothetical Technology Roadmap Summary Chart

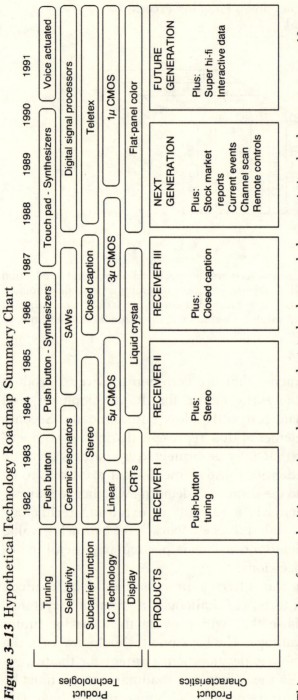

This summary chart for a television receiver shows product technology and characteristics development over a 10-year period. Similar summary documents detail production technology development.

SOURCE: Adapted from C. H. Willyard and C. W. McClees, "Motorola's Technology Roadmap Process," *Research Management,* September–October 1987, p. 18.

structured activity, it is important to avoid being trapped by the details of the process at the expense of the content of the plan.

Unlike business and budget plans, technology roadmaps need not be revised annually. The need to revise or redraw the roadmap is driven more by market and technology changes, which may occur at different paces.

END GAME DECISIONS

As discussed previously, the life of individual products and services is a cycle consisting of development, growth, and decline phases. Each successive product version has improved performance, reduced cost, higher reliability, or other design and production improvements. As new versions of products appear, sales of earlier offerings generally decline as the market shifts to the newer product.

A business consisting of a family of products undergoes a similar cycle, made up of the sum of the product cycles of the family product members. Like individual products, such businesses have a development phase, a growth phase, and, finally, a maturity phase—the end game. Technology-driven and market-driven commercialization activities typically occur during business development phases; a series of product- and process-improvement commercialization efforts provides the driving power for the growth phase. Product- and process-improvement commercialization continues throughout the end game, but maturity has its own special considerations.

During maturity, markets may reach saturation, the rate of technical advance may slow as the cost of incremental performance improvements rises, the number of competitors may drop as successful participants gain established market positions, the product and manufacturing technology becomes generally known, and the cost of entering the business may become prohibitively high for newcomers.

All this paints a picture of market and production stability. The end game can be a phase of excellent return for persistent, successful competitors. It also can be a period of substantial risk.

In the end game, we can see the rise of new technologies or product characteristics that supplant the old ways and establish entirely new approaches to the product, process, or service. The replacement of silk stockings with nylon stockings (between 1938 and 1950) is a good example. It can also be a period during which technical change in other fields can change the requirements of successful competition in confusing ways. For example, the growth of bioengineering in agriculture is likely to have a profound impact on the agricultural tractor business, but it is entirely unclear how the requirements for tractors will change as a result of new crop characteristics and planting patterns.

Understanding when a business approaches maturity and the nature of issues that must be addressed during this phase is critical in successfully dealing with the end game. Managers of businesses approaching the end game face the following critical questions:

- Is the business really approaching maturity, or will the growth phase continue?
- How long can I continue to exploit the current family architecture and production methods before I must look for radically new product ideas?
- If the end game is approaching, should I plan to persist in the business, or am I better off to leave the field under the best possible conditions?

Many nontechnological considerations apply to the end game of business development. For instance, market growth, the nature of competing firms, ability to finance major changes in the business, and the changing environment for the product can be factors. We can add little to these considerations that is not already part of management techniques for other commercialization activities.

There are, however, management tools for anticipating the effect of technological change on the onset of maturity and developing the expectation of the need for change. Prolonged growth of a business dulls the sense of the need for major technological or design shifts. The vulnerability of the American automobile industry to smaller, fuel-efficient foreign products is attributable, in part, to complacency of U.S. producers with the gaudy, high-performance gas-guzzlers of the 1950s and 1960s.

Similarly, computer manufacturers are reluctant to consider new product architectures when the current generation is still selling well. The cost of developing and introducing new product families can be immense. Yet failure to recognize and plan for appropriately timed major product changes can leave a computer firm dead in the water when the momentum of the current product line runs out.

Ability to spot the need for technological revolution in an established business has been the mark of the talented strategic manager. The sense of timing to produce new products that launch into a new realm of performance, application, or cost is often a result of a "visceral feel" for the market and technology. Such visionaries know when to leave the security of the current product growth curve and to leap onto the development curve for a new product family that promises to render earlier products obsolete.

There is a product life cycle analytical tool that can help augment the feel for needed business discontinuities. Modis and Debecker studied the computer industry problem to develop a predictive tool to signal when major changes will be needed.[19] Their technique relies on the observation that the life cycle of a family of products often follows a mathematical function called the "logistic curve." Specifically, this curve is a good fit to the number of models in a computer product family based on a given computer architecture. (It also fits many other indices of product life, such as sales.) By mathematically fitting early product experience to the logistical function, Modis and Debecker can estimate the onset of maturity for a given computer company's product line, and the needed timing for new product architectures.

Included in their paper are examples of some product lines

that had unexpectedly matured early. Still others, just as unexpectedly, had much farther to go before reaching the end game. Modis and Debecker's method has been applied to other product families and may be a useful predictor of the need for revision of fundamental product concepts.

Other businesses are unlikely to be supplanted by newer product ideas. The electronic vacuum tube business was done in by transistors, and later, integrated circuits. Yet discrete transistors, the oldest semiconductor products, remain a growing business that has provided a generous return for the remaining, successful firms. The reason is that discrete semiconductor devices can have some critical characteristics that integrated circuits have been unable to match, such as higher breakdown voltage, maximum current capability, power-handling ability, and cutoff frequency. The discrete semiconductor business remains an indispensable part of the electronic components business.

The need for continuous assessment of the risk of new technology and product threats to existing businesses is particularly great in the end game of product life. In earlier phases of business development, rapid growth allows flexibility for new competitors and new ideas to enter the business. Growth phase businesses often are tolerant of slow reaction to change because there is growth enough in the market to cushion the error. In the end game, slower growth makes for a much more brittle situation. When many consider a business to be a "given" is when it can be most vulnerable to technological surprise attack.

4

A New Order of Things

Organization and Management of Commercialization Activities

There is nothing more difficult to take in hand, more perilous to conduct, or more uncertain in its success, than to take the lead in the introduction of a new order of things.

N. MACHIAVELLI, *The Prince*

A pervasive and resilient misperception about technological progress is that it results from a simple progression of events beginning with discovery of laws of nature, followed by invention of their uses, then by application development, and ending with the design and refinement of a production process or manufactured product. Were this simple, linear model correct and widely applicable, it would be an easy matter to organize businesses to develop and exploit technology. Management challenges would consist of moving ideas along an assembly line made up of departments of research, design and development, and production.

In practice, technological change is a much less well defined, iterative, and uncertain process—it is often nonlinear.
Effective new technology development, its insertion into new
product and process developments, and its incorporation
into existing products and production processes require that
the technology evolve to suit the application as it progresses
from conception to verification and on to employment. This
evolutionary process is part learning and part doing, a process usually carried out by technical personnel, often working in close contact with others with complementary
expertise. The refinement and selection of technological opportunities must be handled close to applications that have
value for the ultimate customer. Important aspects of new
technology must be developed, tested, and refined throughout an organization, not just in the research and development laboratory. Not surprisingly, these characteristics of
technological advance have important implications for effective organization and management. Businesses that ex-
pect to be successful commercializing new products and
processes must develop organizations and management
practices that can handle and direct the necessary learning.

Perhaps the single most important insight about managing technology commercialization is that product and service realization issues must be tackled *concurrently*.
Commercialization must be seen as a *single business activity*
from beginning to end. Its successful pursuit requires commitment of all involved people and management levels. The
product realization process must be thought of as the design
and implementation of a complete system—including the
product or service, its application, the production process,
marketing, and distribution and support activity. Quality,
manufacturability, maintainability, and ability to respond
to customer feedback must be addressed up front, as the
product or service is taking shape, and not as afterthoughts
when production begins.

Management must think of product and process innovation as a whole-company activity that focuses on continuous
improvement in the value delivered to the customer, all the

while using fewer resources and working faster than competitors. With that goal firmly in mind, research, product design, manufacturing, marketing, distribution, and service are all crucial functions in effective commercial innovation. As such, they need to be managed, and sometimes organized, as a single system.

It is beyond the scope of this book to address all knowledge, folklore, best practices, and myths about organization and management of business enterprises. This chapter focuses on identifying and discussing a few important organizational and management challenges in the commercialization of new products and processes.

CHALLENGE ONE: BALANCING FOCUS AND DISORDER, PROMOTING INTELLIGENT RISK TAKING AND EXPERIMENTATION

Focus and disorder must be balanced in a company's technological activities. Progress arises out of a tension between the sometimes disordered forces of creative problem solving and the focus necessary to carry an idea to completion. The creative process involves some unprogrammed effort to support experimentation and the search for solutions to new problems. Focus, of course, is essential to keep the effort moving forward in a direction consistent with company goals, but too much control can kill innovative potential. Since risk and experimentation are at the heart of most businesses' technological activities, part of the challenge of managing technology is to promote useful experimentation, yet manage risk.

A manager focused on profiting from innovation has to accept that the search for technological solutions is usually a disorderly trial-and-error process. At its core, it is inherently wasteful. Wrong turns are endemic, as discussed by Rosabeth Moss Kanter:

In nearly every change project, doubt is cast on the original vision because problems are mounting and the end is nowhere in sight. Resources have been expended without the ability to demonstrate when there might be a return.

There are four main sources of this "vulnerability of the mid-stages," well illustrated by numerous small-scale innovations, as well as large efforts such as the IBM 360 development:

1. *Forecasting problems.* The project runs out of time or resources because of overoptimistic forecasts ("it's costing $40 million—now $50 million—now $60 million . . . ."), themselves a function of the enormous uncertainties inherent in innovation and change.

2. *Unexpected obstacles.* The project hits bottlenecks, technological roadblocks or "unscheduled developments"—which mostly could not have been foreseen because there is no experience base to know they might be there.

3. *Critics surface.* Although there may be resistance at all stages, resistance is likelier once the project is well under way and looks as if it might succeed, because then the threat changes from an intellectual matter to a tangible matter—hey, this might actually happen.

4. *Working teams lose momentum.* Change is, after all, hard work, and results are not instantaneous or guaranteed. After the euphoria of beginnings, when awareness of a special mission is highly motivating, middles can seem like an endless series of disappointments and thankless tasks.[1]

Technological innovation in companies has a special logic, a logic that may lead to a set of management behaviors that differ from what would be considered "good management practice." In particular, technological innovation requires intelligent experimentation. Experimentation, of course, requires investment of resources in activities designed so that *failure is acceptable as long as it provides useful information about what is and is not possible.* Although many large corporate laboratories have developed such a culture, it is a courageous (read foolhardy and unrewarded) line manager who will commit resources to such an activity. Yet technological innovation relies on information from intelligent experiments. Through such trials, engineers and technologists often discover the full range of techniques needed for application—both critical and ancillary—that no one thought about during laboratory development. Managers who seriously take the charge to use technology effectively must find a way to encourage and learn from technological experimentation and to do it rapidly.

A corporation's own bureaucracy—often designed to control decisions and expenditures—can be the most serious impediment to technical advance. James Brian Quinn characterized the challenge as follows:

> Progress in technology is largely determined by the number of successful experiments made per unit time. Skunkworks help eliminate bureaucratic delays, allow fast unfettered communication, and permit the quick turnarounds and decisions that stimulate rapid advance. . . . By keeping total division sizes below 400, close communications can be maintained with only two intervening decision layers to the top. In units much larger than this, people quickly lose touch with the total concept of their product or process, bureaucracies grow, and projects must go through more and more formal screens to survive. Since it takes a chain of "yeses" to approve a project as it moves to the top and only one "no" to kill it, jeopardy multiplies as management layers increase.[2]

If a company cannot bring itself to try something new—to experiment quickly to learn what is technologically possible—it is likely to be beaten in the marketplace by those willing to act faster and take the risk. A company that wants to advance technologically must reward, not punish, risk-taking and entrepreneurial behavior. Adventurous champions and teams must be tolerated and nurtured.

The management challenge of balancing focus and disorder is not trivial. A manager must maintain a long-term dedication and a commitment to the goals of the organization and be willing to make timely decisions, set priorities, and establish and enforce project goals. All the while he or she must stomach the fits and starts of technological processes. It is a difficult task, and the challenges it presents have important implications for organizational design, for the processes used to set and pursue goals, and for personnel practices.

CHALLENGE TWO: NURTURING CHAMPIONS

Success. Four flights Thursday morning. All against twenty-one mile wind. Started from level with engine power alone. Average speed through air thirty-one miles. Longest fifty-nine seconds. Inform press. Home Christmas.

Telegram from Wilbur and Orville Wright to the
Reverend Milton Wright, December 17, 1903

Project or technology champions are particularly important to commercialization success across a wide range of industries. Perhaps the primary characteristic of champions is that they accept responsibility both for the focus of their enterprise and for its success or failure. They become personally invested in, and identify with, pushing whatever piece of the world they can control to introduce a product, install a manufacturing process, promote a key business attribute (such as total quality control), or apply an innovative idea. The attributes of technical or entrepreneurial pioneers often include a deep and abiding personal paradox—at the same time that they carry a long-term vision of a market, they do not do much early planning. In other words, they manage to look to the future and avoid identifying (or listening to) "why it won't work."

Champions who take charge of an effort and leave their mark on a specific product are lionized in the history of innovation. Examples include Edison for the electric light, Bell for the telephone, and Land for instant photography. Although technical champions play a recognized role in bringing technically novel products and services to market, they can and do contribute to other types of commercialization. A well-chosen and effective champion can focus and intensify team efforts dedicated to market-driven commercialization problems or to product and process improvement.

Champions occur in all guises. Sometimes they are small company entrepreneurs, sometimes senior executives, or, often, they are imbedded in the structure of large companies. Their professional functions vary. They may be managers, researchers, product designers, manufacturing workers, or marketers. Despite these differences, champions share the following important attributes:

- Dedication (sometimes fanatical) to their perception of success, sometimes without management support
- A vision of the goal that is clear enough and powerful enough to enlist the support of others
- Willingness to take risks, often personal as well as professional, to reach the goal
- Ability to garner sufficient resources (through leadership, management insight, "reappropriation," persuasion, luck, or intuition) to reach the goal

Champions' activities often do not conform to formal organizations or "orderly" ways of doing business. Though company leaders may wish to encourage champions throughout their firm, they often fail to recognize, empower, and reward "constructive" disruptive behavior. On the other hand, it is also true that among the many individuals who believe fervently in what they are doing, only a few have the breadth of view, energy, and insight necessary to select and champion an important technological advance. The challenge to management is to select and nurture champions who have a reasonable chance of success, given the competence, limitations, and orientation of the company.

An important aspect of a senior executive's job lies in establishing an atmosphere that fosters champions to ensure the long-term growth of the business. He or she also needs to have enough background and understanding of the business, as well as enough personal effectiveness, to be able to champion the champion in the executive suite. Resources must be available to nurture championed activities, and that responsibility lies with top management.

CHALLENGE THREE: BUILDING A USEFUL TECHNOLOGICAL INFORMATION SYSTEM

The cost and complexity of technology needed to succeed in a business have escalated beyond the abilities of many individual companies. Within a single field, basic research may be done in universities; research and advanced product development in an industry consortium; and manufacturing in the product departments of competing companies. In such a technologically disintegrated structure, it can be very difficult to maintain the continuous improvement in products and processes required for success throughout their lives with internal resources alone.

Luckily, besides its own technical resources, each firm can draw on a network of organizations to resolve questions about applications of both simple and complex innovations. Confronted with technological challenges, a company has a variety of options: hire new personnel with the insight and training to evaluate and implement innovations, seek information about technological advances from suppliers, hire consultants, or use testing laboratories. In other words, there is an extensive network of information providers.

The downside, of course, is that competitors have access to the same information. They buy equipment from the same suppliers, their engineers belong to the same professional societies and read the same publications, and they interact with the same educational institutions in hope of attracting good technical talent. In a developed, technically complex industrial economy, corporations share a set of scientific and technological resources.

Availability of the external resources is not what differentiates firm performance in accessing, acquiring, and applying technology. It is the ability of the firm to make effective use of the available resources. There are no generic solutions—the approach to acquiring a technology depends on the specific needs of the company—but there are two important sets of resources. First, the technological search and acquisition process should be led by someone knowledgeable both about the range of technological opportunities and about the needs of the business. The second resource necessary for the acquisition of technology is something to trade. A firm must be willing to trade for, or pay for, access to new technologies. Frequently, money to buy a technology is not the issue. It may be necessary to trade technology for technology, establish a joint venture, trade licenses or patents, or make another type of "I'll tell you how to do this if you'll tell me how to do that" arrangement. There is no simple recipe that translates money or technological capability in one area into technological capability in new areas. The specific form of a trade—and the value of that trade to a corporation—is determined by the imagination, insight, and persistence of the parties involved.

The two types of resources—technologically sophisticated personnel and something to trade—allow a business to stay abreast of the state of scientific and engineering knowledge for a company's products or processes, and to get technological capability that does not exist within the firm. In this context, the importance of person-to-person contact cannot be overestimated.

Publication (in technological fields) occupies a position of less importance than it does in science where it serves to document results and establish priority. Because published information is at best secondary to the actual utilization of the technical innovation, this archival function is not as essential to ensure the reputation of a technologist. We do not remember the names of Wilbur and Orville Wright because they published papers. . . . The technologist's principal legacy is encoded in physical, not verbal, structure. So the technologist publishes less and devotes less time to reading than do scientists. Information transfer in technology is primarily through personal contact.[3]

Technological advance is a human endeavor, and people are the primary link between what is theoretically possible and what happens in the laboratory, in the design shop, or on the plant floor. People involved with technology may fail to document a discovery because once the system is working, there is little incentive or time to document the solution. The importance of formal systems for recording and documenting technology varies substantially by industry and technology, but in virtually every industry people are the "carriers" of technological knowledge. Documentation is often done primarily for internal technology transfer and later field service.

As a result, the scientific and engineering community concerned with technologies close to the heart of the products and processes is perhaps the most important single source of general technical information about an industry. In this light, the professional community of a company's technical personnel is an invaluable resource. No professional network knows about every technology, but it is usually possible for a determined technical professional to discover much of the information available. The tools for this discovery are well known—personal and professional contacts, conferences, and the technical and trade literature. Yet the integration of a company's technical personnel into its professional community is often underrated as a fundamental business information system. In the United States, professional societies— through their publications and conferences—are the primary organizational mechanisms by which technical personnel in business interact with their professional communities.

There is no shortage of professional societies in the United States. The most recent *Directory of Engineering Societies,*[4] published by the American Association of Engineering Societies, lists 360 U.S. national and international organizations that are primarily engineering oriented or have activities related to engineering. These societies publish many technical journals and sponsor thousands of technical conferences each year. Societies range in size and activity from the international Institute of Electrical and Electronics Engineers (almost a quarter of a million members, publishing 37 periodicals and more than 50,000 conference reports, records, and standards each year) to the Society for Computer Simulation (with about 3,500 members, publishing a bimonthly periodical and a semiannual report). The professional science and engineering literature is an important source of information within a technical community, as is trade literature that can provide useful clues about what others are working on.

Attendance at technical conferences is another opportunity for a company's professionals to meet colleagues from universities and other companies in an atmosphere where technical "gossip" can provide useful information about developing technological areas. Such informal contacts can be more important than the papers presented, since they are likely to give more up-to-date, albeit less detailed, information. The key to effective access to the information content of technical conferences is the ability of attenders to make a contribution to the field. An observer, no matter how knowledgeable, will be a less effective gatherer of information than an active researcher would be. Information trading is at the heart of technical conferences, and trading requires a willingness to give information in exchange for new information. Access to technical advances *requires* familiarity with the technical field, the professional community, and with the literature.

The external technical advisory committee is another way in which firms can search for general technical knowledge. Such a committee engages individuals from outside the firm in the firm's technological activities. Any firm with the resources can create such a group, the most effective of which comprise exceptionally competent outsiders who would be impossible for the firm to hire. Technical advisory committees, besides providing insights about current internal problems, can be a source of contacts with technology networks beyond the firm. They can provide an additional source of "early warning" about technological developments, and a way of learning about subjects that may be new to the firm.

Finally, university faculty can be an important technical resource for firms. Engineering schools and their faculty usually welcome contact with industrial technologists interested in, and knowledgeable about, technological frontiers. Consulting relationships with individual faculty members can provide an excellent window into developing fields of knowledge at their frontier, provide useful collaborators in research and development, and be a source for entry into broader technological networks. Many universities have organized industrial consortia and advisory committees that enable firms to participate in such contacts with other firms in a way that makes it less expensive than exclusive sponsorship of research.

These arrangements provide a possible source of consultants on particular subjects, and, through contacts with students, a source of new recruits for the firm. This often entails expenditure of money, but more important, the time of one or more of the firm's technologists to work with the university if the contacts are to be of use.

In sum, management policies and organizational structures designed to drive development, acquisition, and use of technology must reflect the human nature of technological knowledge if they are to succeed. The kind of intimacy needed among the various parties to the successful transfer of technology has implications for how a firm should operate.

CHALLENGE FOUR:
MANAGING JOINT TECHNOLOGY EFFORTS

Another way for organizations to acquire a particular technological capability is for people who want the technology to work side by side with people who have it. Licenses, supplier arrangements, joint ventures, acquisitions, and research consortia are mechanisms by which companies bring together technical personnel for exchange of technology.

There are many ways in which a company can acquire a specific capability. Joint ventures for the production of a specific product, cooperative product development arrangements, research consortia, or acquisition all have potential. Firms that are not direct competitors can have common or interlocking technological needs. There are few, if any, general rules guiding joint activities for development of technological capability. Partnerships and alliances for specific research, development, production, or distribution are among the most important opportunities for gaining technological capability from outside the company.

Novel technological alliances are assuming greater importance as the complexity and scope of American business increase. Besides unconventional purchasing relationships, these alliances now include technology transfer agreements with other companies, universities and government entities, and technology development consortia, and include product design contracts, production relationships, and marketing agreements. Partnerships provide important options for company strategy.

Alliances may take many forms. Purchasing agreements are the most common, but joint development, technology transfer, licensing, joint venture, and minority ownership arrangements are popular. Still, many American companies have had unfavorable experiences with "partnership" relationships. This stands in clear contrast to the operating style of firms in a few countries, particularly Japan. This is partly a reflection of differences between nations in financing and ownership, yet a more important difference lies in the manner in which participating companies manage major partnerships. Successful partnerships require that management consider the broader context of the relationship.

Partnerships should be established with the premise that all parties must benefit from the alliance. Agreements that develop into winner/loser situations self-destruct, often in ways that damage both partners. The following three practices can help avoid partnership failures:

- Partnerships should arise from an understanding between senior officials in the collaborating organizations.
- All relevant parties in each allied organization should understand and be willing to support the partnership before agreement between senior officials. The internal process of reaching agreement on the execution of an alliance can be a more difficult negotiation than the external agreement itself.
- Execution of partnership arrangements should not be completely delegated to less senior personnel, whose comprehension of the agreement and its context, and whose objectives and authority, differ significantly from those of the original negotiators.

Consortia are another partnership option. Under the Cooperative Research and Development Act of 1984, competitors can now join in a consortium to do common pre-competitive research. The semiconductor consortium SEMATECH has even pioneered in the use of consortia to develop manufacturing technology. Corsortia can be attractive wherever the costs of technology development strain the ability of single companies to support developments needed to continue their businesses. Experience with the Microelectronics and Computer Technology Corporation (MCC) shows that consortium arrangements can grant each participant access to research results equal to or substantially greater than its investment and that these are an attractive opportunity for U.S. corporations.

This large a multiple is necessary because the costs of partnership go well beyond those of direct support to the joint effort itself. All partners to an agreement must be prepared, from the outset, to commit themselves to making the agreement work. Successful participants in technology consortia, for example, are those who establish an internal "shadow" cadre to track the activities of the joint effort. This group figures out how best to use it to further the company's goals, and prepares for implementation of the technology. Such a firm can then use the fruits of the collaborative research when they are available—a significant advantage over those partners who wait for results to arrive before tackling the technology transfer process.

Successful commercial appliers of the fruits of academic and government developments adopt similar approaches to managing the transfer. They assign employees to spend time in university or government labs to become immersed in development work. A similar method appears to work well in managing the relationship between a company and a consortium.

Internal shadow operations to track common technology development efforts are a hidden cost of participation in consortia and other R&D pooling arrangements. These hidden costs should be recognized up front when planning the agreement if companies are to understand accurately the extent of their participation.

Finally, just as with other aspects of company strategy, partnerships eventually reach the end of their useful life—when the partners go their own way. For this reason, provisions for orderly dissolution of alliances should be considered at formation, before the pressures to separate dominate thinking. Establishing terms of the "end game" up front does not preclude the possibility of follow-on relationships, but allows the parties to plan for an orderly disengagement. Managers will be continuously challenged to come up with creative ways to stay in touch with technological advances outside their companies, forming teams with common goals involving suppliers, customers, and other involved organizations and to manage a successful exit should it become necessary to break off a business relationship.

CHALLENGE FIVE: ORGANIZING TO DEVELOP NEW TECHNOLOGY TO CREATE NEW BUSINESSES

Use of a new technology, or new application of a technology, to create a truly new product, process, or service (what we have called technology-driven or market-driven commercialization) creates special demands on a company. As shown in Figure 4–1, project progress from concept to marketplace takes place in a series of stages. There is a somewhat linear organizational logic to the development of such a technology-based business. It begins with development of a new idea (within or outside of a laboratory, inside or outside of a company) and moves through a series of tests of technical and market feasibility, manufacturability, and commercial validation to production and support. Each stage can demand different competencies from members of a "project team." The process is often iterative, with new products, processes, or services moving forward, only to revert to an earlier stage to deal with unanticipated problems. Not surprisingly, the transfer of technical and market information between project teams within established departments of a company is an important challenge to the creation of new technology-based businesses.

Figure 4–1 Formulation of Multispecialty Project Team Designed to Accomplish Simultaneous Engineering in the Stages

Stage 1	Stage 2	Stage 3	Stage 4	Stage 5	Stage 6
Conceptual	Technical Feasibility	Development	Commercial Validation & Production Preparation	Full-Scale Production	Product Support
Project Team *Inventor Research engineer	Project Team *Research engineer Development engineer Marketing/ business Manufacturing engineer	Project Team *Development eng'r Manufacturing engineer Test engineer Mktg/cost estimator	Project Team *Design engineer Test engineer Manucturing engineer Development engineer Buyer Q&A eng'r Marketing	Project Team *Manufacturing engineer Q&A eng'r Test engineer Construction engineer Process engineer Marketing Sales Product cost analyst Buyer Suppliers	Project Team *Marketing Sales Q&A Training Distributors Product improvement Survey Field service Suppliers

*Possible project team manager or product champion of stage.

SOURCE: National Society of Professional Engineers, *Engineering Stages of New Product Development* (Alexandria, Va.: NSPE, 1990). Reprinted by permission of the Society of Professional Engineers.

Enterprises facing technology-driven or dramatic new market-driven commercialization challenges can make effective use of traditional sequential organization structures (such as that shown in Figure 4–2), though there are often concerns about contributors being too disconnected from each other. In these structures, responsibility for a commercialization project is passed between teams associated with fixed company departments. Several factors mitigate the typical shortcomings of linear organizations in dealing with significant technological change. The technology-driven or dramatic market-driven commercialization effort stretches over many years, so time pressure is not as great a problem as it is for other commercialization types. The specific application of the technology in question is often uncertain. Because several distinct market opportunities might be envisioned, the organization may branch from a single research lab to several application-specific groups, each focusing on a particular market segment. Revolutionary technology opportunities may begin as scientific discoveries with few known practical product or process design techniques. Significant supporting inventions and technology adaptation may, therefore, be necessary to bring the product to market. In such cases, the more people engaged in supporting the

Figure 4–2 Traditional Commercialization Model

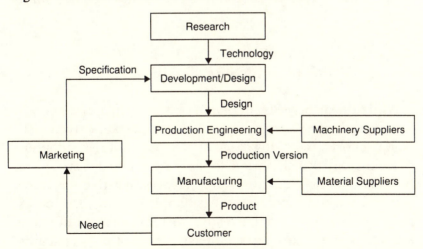

original idea, the better the chance of finding meaningful supporting inventions. Finally, because the revolutionary idea may have originated outside the company's control, a linear structure may be required to connect internal operations to external ones.

There are, however, significant risks in linear organizations even for technology-driven projects. Because activities take place sequentially, the process is slow—perhaps beyond the attention span of middle and senior management—and failure to transfer technology at any point along the way jeopardizes the entire undertaking. In the linear "bucket brigade," ability to transfer technology accurately and quickly between organizations is crucial. An especially vulnerable point in the deployment of a new technology is where responsibility passes from research to operations.

Often, companies seeking to minimize technology transfer problems between internal organizations periodically shift responsibility for directing critical departments from functional research departments to integrated production and development managers and back. The hope is to balance long-range and near-term concerns. Each management approach has its advantages and limitations. It is not hard to reach the conclusion that periodic change is the best scheme to deal with technology development and deployment problems in businesses undergoing rapid technological change.

CHALLENGE SIX: BUILDING
MORE RESPONSIVE PROJECT TEAMS

While linear organizations may be an appropriate choice for revolutionary technology-driven and market-driven technology efforts, their slow pace of progress and risks inherent in technology transfer argue for a more responsive structure. In most commercialization projects, competitive pressures demand a more rapid, lower risk approach. In these cases, practitioners of technology have to be where applications are taking place; this drives the structure of project teams.

"Floating" project teams, focused on a specific design, process, or technology and not attached to a single functional department, are important in many market-driven developments and in product- and process-improvement commercialization efforts. Such project teams are separate groups, set aside to carry out a clearly defined task. As illustrated in Figure 4–3, they must interact with virtually every functional organization in the firm to accomplish their goals. Depending on the industry and company, this can mean reassignment (temporary or permanent) of key people as activities associated with a product, process, or service development change. The membership of such dynamic, project-oriented organizations changes with time as the focus of the group shifts to confront successive technology application stages. Membership in such teams may be quite flexible and may even include suppliers, customers, consultants, and members of technical advisory groups as needed.

Project-oriented organizations are characteristic of firms, such as defense contractors and the construction industry,

Figure 4–3 Project Team Commercialization Model

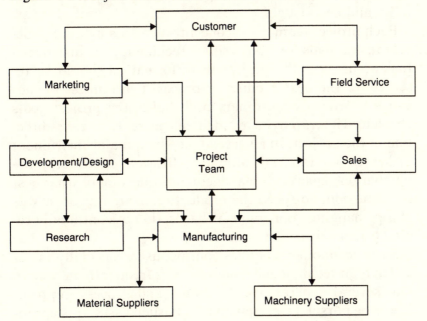

whose principal product is the sale of engineering services. They have not been as widely used in medium-to-large product or service companies. Many small companies are the equivalent of single project-oriented teams because of the need to concentrate all resources on a single goal. In project team situations, the ability to develop and apply technology relies on bringing needed skills to bear on the problem by assignment of key people. The exact mix of skills embodied in such coalitions changes with time as requirements shift. The fixed, functional parts of the company (such as R&D labs, product design departments, and manufacturing engineering) remain in place as the conservators of expertise in the specific skills needed for the wide range of activities to be undertaken in technology development and application.

This dynamic organizational approach to technology development reduces technology transfer because the project organization itself evolves to adapt to each stage in the application process; technology transfers to other organizations are minimized, as the project team stays on the job from beginning to end. Thus, technology transfer is not an issue, and time is not lost in transferring project responsibility and knowledge.

Each project team must concentrate on a single set of development goals for best results. Technology advancements that occur after the project team formation should be reserved for the next product or process team unless the advance is truly extraordinary and makes the project goals obsolete. The trap to be avoided, of course, is costly redirection of the project. In a survey taken by a major instrument maker in its internal commercialization operations, the number one answer to management's question of what best could be done to speed the product realization process was "Stop changing your mind." That is, do not continually redirect the goals of the project.

Since technology changes continuously, especially in so-called high-technology businesses, it is frequently necessary that several generations of product and process improvements be pursued simultaneously. In such cases, it is appropriate to form multiple project groups, each to focus on a single evolutionary step. Although such approaches can be effective, there are drawbacks. In particular, the existence of multiple project groups can diffuse company goals and create tensions; the continuous organizational changes necessarily associated with this type of coalition can be viewed by participants as a threat. The unknowns of where the next assignment will come from, keeping personnel up to date with the latest technology developments in their specialty areas, and the management problems of dealing with changing company needs can be deeply unsettling—a major burden both to the people within the organization and especially to company leaders who have to maintain forward momentum in the organization.

In a rapidly changing, and sometimes seemingly chaotic, corporate environment, traditional fixed "functional" groups (such as R&D, design, manufacturing engineering, marketing, and so on) are the permanent homes for assigned personnel. They serve to bring the latest techniques in their focus area into the company. When a project team requires expertise in a specific area, it must borrow (sometimes for an extended period) from functional organizations to meet its needs. As the focus of the project shifts, and the services of practitioners of a particular specialty are no longer required, those people return to their permanent billet to renew their skills. Thus the dual needs of skill replenishment and organizational stability are served.

An alternative approach to managing technology transfers between organizations involves temporary reassignment of personnel between transferring and receiving groups. Although this technique satisfies the dictum that "technology moves best when people move too," knowledge that the assignment is likely to be brief and that responsibility for the future of the product or process is likely to end soon can cause assignees to adopt a short-timer approach to the success of the overall project.

In spite of its inherent advantages, a project team organization will perform inefficiently if project goals are moving targets. If, as a project progresses, new or changed specifications are periodically added to the purpose and design of the product, the group effort may wander from one project review to the next and fail to converge on a desired result. This effect, termed "feature creep" by some insightful people at the Hewlett-Packard company, can effectively delay conclusion of a commercialization effort. Management must have the discipline to see a project through to conclusion unless major shifts in market or technology occur, in which case the effort should often be restarted.

CHALLENGE SEVEN: USING A PROJECT CONTRACT TO DRIVE COMMERCIALIZATION

Success in product- and process-improvement commercialization depends on speed and error-free performance. Technology risks are modest, as are market risks, because of prior experience in the market. In such cases, time is an important factor in commercialization success. Being first to enter a market with a well-designed, attractive product—or being early in the use of an important process advance—can create extremely important long-term advantages. The need for speed in commercialization does not, however, lessen the need for coordination and planning in executing all the tasks needed to bring a product to market or process to production use. Quite the opposite. False starts, where products introduced to the market must be called back to correct design or production flaws, are usually worse than being late. Instead, emphasis on speed of execution means using those planning, goal-setting, and organizational techniques that help the project to progress.

As described earlier, task teams with clear objectives, which balance organizational stability and flexibility throughout the development and manufacturing life of a product or process, may be in the best position to speed the flow of technology from research to practice. But those teams need an effective organizational mechanism for coordinating and driving their work. Without a constructive method of planning and coordinating the various actors in a project, problems show up quickly. For example, poorly managed development processes can have product and process designs "thrown over the wall" from development departments to production and marketing organizations at the conclusion of successful design efforts, only to fail commercially. In such cases, all parties disavow responsibility for fixing problems and making future improvements. Stalemate is assured, and progress becomes the victim of conflicting goals.

The initial effort required to establish a sound plan can be a time-consuming process, but time and effort taken to understand the project from the start can be recovered manyfold in improved execution. Discipline is required to ensure that the plan remains in effect yet flexible so that the goals remain consistent while allowing the terms and conditions of work to change as initial assumptions prove flawed or false. The establishment of a working "contract" (not a legal contract, but a formal understanding) between the several parties to the development project is one useful mechanism for forming and directing the work of multidisciplinary commercialization teams. Such a contract should establish goals, schedules, detailed specifications, and resources required for the effort.

Parties to such contracts should include marketing (which agrees to a product specification it commits to sell), development (which commits to a product or process specification and schedule to which it can design), production (which agrees to design rules, production volume, and schedules it can meet), and management (which commits to provide resources called for in the contract, as long as other commitments are met).

The concept goes beyond the traditional project plan in that the contract is created within the project team itself. It embodies an agreement among the various elements of the team. Such a formalism must be sufficiently well thought out from the start that substantive changes are unlikely unless major shifts in initial assumptions occur. Consistent and documented goals contained in such internal contracts, whether formal or informal, help provide an atmosphere in which project planning assumptions remain valid, and progress against milestones can be measured. At the same time that the contract sets the direction and makes clear expectations, it is not intended to be a "sign-it-and-forget-it" event for either team members or management. Effective management of technological developments requires constant and competent review and status assessment to track progress and involve senior management in any decisions that affect fundamental direction of the project.

Depending on the specific character of the project, there are many opportunities for review—for seeing that the terms of the contract remain valid and that the project is on course. Businesses have a virtually unlimited number of regular opportunities to check the status of internal contracts or agreements. For some product- and process-improvement commercialization projects, natural review opportunities may include the following:

- Routinely scheduled meetings—e.g., staff meetings, performance reviews, employee participation meetings
- The weekly, monthly, quarterly, and annual financial cycles—e.g., budgets and performance figures
- Project meetings—e.g., meetings to discuss, agree on, and coordinate actions among participants
- Production facility decisions—e.g., decisions taken to replace, change, or upgrade production equipment

In a business not in crisis, these regular patterns are the mechanisms for change and action, including technological change. The contract and review process is the way in which technological ideas, notions, and visions are translated into organizational form, a crucial translation since it is the business unit, not the technology itself, that must profit.

As a final point, the importance of constancy of purpose on the part of senior management—the willingness of management to live up to its end of a contract—cannot be overemphasized and is illustrated by the story of development of three-dimensional computer-aided design (3-D CAD) technology at the Bechtel Corporation.

Bechtel, like many global engineering and construction firms, is organized around project teams and areas of the world. By 1982 several Bechtel organizations had effectively developed CAD technology in the automation of 2-D drafting tasks. For each project, Bechtel typically produces numerous drawings representing the facility's arrangement and the design of systems, equipment, piping, cabling, instruments, and other components. Initially, the company treated CAD as a special service to the projects, and specialists outside of project organizations managed and operated it. During the early 1980s it was becoming clear that the trend would be to bring CAD tools to the projects where designers and engineers, not CAD specialists, would become productive users of the automation in day-to-day activities. In addition, several technical engineering personnel recognized the potential of CAD beyond that of 2-D drafting. They saw that 3-D computer modeling, along with appropriate electronic data bases, could help broader project objectives such as planning, engineering, and construction activities.

The development process was kicked off when one of Bechtel's engineering technical groups proposed an internal development of a comprehensive and Bechtel-specific 3-D design system. Engineering management in one of the operating companies approved the project, and the development team was set up and launched in a very low-profile way. Within six months, the development project had progressed to the point that project testing could begin. Although there were bugs in the design system, during its initial project test on a condensate polishing facility at a nuclear plant site, the 3-D model did identify design discrepancies and interferences and cut by 75 percent the job hours required for a crucial redesign.

Immediately following the initial test, other project groups became interested in applying the new 3-D system. The project groups and engineering management worked together closely to establish the necessary support to accommodate the new demands. The early projects risked schedule and cost commitments by abandoning established engineering and design methods in favor of the new 3-D methods. There were many training and start-up problems, but the groups worked together to resolve these issues quickly. Their determination paid off in higher quality and quicker design products. These early successes were communicated throughout Bechtel, and the 3-D software was distributed to all design offices. Later the managers of engineering from each office met in San Francisco to establish this 3-D system as a Bechtel standard for all projects.

Since that success, the use of automation has grown in Bechtel, as reflected in use of the tools and in organizational changes such as the establishment of an Engineering and Construction Technologies Department within Research and Development, the creation of operating centers within the engineering departments for management of CAD computer equipment, and the creation of Bechtel Software, Inc., chartered to market, sell, and distribute innovative Bechtel software applications. Such dramatic technical and business developments do not take place without substantial coordination and commitment on the part of management. At each stage of the development—first of the new technology and then of new businesses—project team members involved with the development recognized the commitment of the company's management to the projects. A tolerant and supportive management—a management that lived up to its contracts—

was a crucial success factor in bringing design tools
for construction into use in Bechtel.[5]

Both aspects of the process—the "get-ready" or contract-
ing effort and the ongoing review and status assessment
activities—of commercialization are extremely important to
ultimate success. Whether the product of the get-ready activity is a formal understanding or not, a good start is one of
the most important things a manager can do to ensure successful commercialization.

CHALLENGE EIGHT: INTEGRATING CORPORATE TECHNICAL EFFORTS

Earlier challenges have focused on ways to organize commercialization project activities. Project organizations come
and go with changes in tasks to be done. Many medium-size
and large companies also must have some fixed structure in
the firm. In contrast to project organizations, these fixed
organizations have functional responsibilities. As noted earlier, they may be the source of staff for ever-shifting project
teams. Functional groups are the center of expertise for specific skills in the firm. These skills can include research and
development, computer aids to design and manufacturing,
strategic marketing, manufacturing tooling, and a host of
other capabilities that do not fit well into more mobile
project organizations. Without functional expertise, the firm
lacks the core knowledge needed to look beyond specific
problems of the moment to capabilities to support future
developments.

Functional organizations frequently develop a life of their
own and lose sight of the continuity needed to make company commercialization a success. Barriers can arise between specialist groups, making it difficult for them to work
together toward common objectives. Stories of new product
designs "thrown over the wall" from the design department
to a manufacturing department unable to manufacture them
are common to many industries.

Identifying and eliminating barriers is a critical task for company leaders. They must be prepared to understand where company objectives are frustrated because of failure of departments to work together—where the gears of company machinery do not mesh properly. Leaders must also be prepared to experiment with changes of management or reorganization to eliminate or reduce obstacles to company progress.

The learning process needed to deal with company functional organizations is illustrated by the development of R&D and production departments in Fairchild Camera and Instrument Corporation and the Intel Corporation. Both companies were in the same business (semiconductor device manufacturing) and each operated under the same managers in successive decades (the 1950s and 1960s for Fairchild and the 1970s and 1980s for Intel).

Fairchild was a pioneer of the semiconductor industry. Robert Noyce invented the silicon planar integrated circuit there in 1958. Fairchild logic and linear integrated circuit products were industry standards during the 1960s, and the staff at the company's Palo Alto R&D Center was responsible for the seminal work that made metal-oxide semiconductor (MOS) device technology a production reality. Ironically, Fairchild was unable to transfer successfully the outstanding technical accomplishments of its research staff to its production operation in Mountain View, a few miles down the road. As a result, Fairchild never competed effectively in the MOS integrated circuit business. Others in the industry put the results of Fairchild's research into practice far more effectively.

Much of this was a result of the organization of Fairchild's technology commercialization activities. The research operation, physically separated from production, was organizationally separate as well. A significant gap existed between the capabilities and resources of the research team and the production staff. The production people, beset by the daily pressures and inertia of volume manufacturing and customer demands, had little time for new ideas and less incentive to consider them seriously. The research and development staff, on the other hand, knowing that they had cut the Gordian knot of an important device technology, was preoccupied with extension of results, rather than scaling them to the needs of mass production. The two groups had great difficulty communicating; neither seemed to speak the other's language. Transfers of people between the two organizations were rare, and reassignments from Palo Alto to Mountain View were viewed as a fall from grace.

The gap that developed between the R&D effort and product operations widened to the point that little real transmission of useful technology took place between the two. Meanwhile, competing firms were hard at work applying Fairchild's new technology, gleaned and extrapolated from the open literature or from ex-Fairchild employees, and building their businesses. Many start-up companies that formed the core of the "Silicon Valley" phenomenon were established and staffed by Fairchild alumni. Many of them beat Fairchild to the market with similar products.

Armed with their experience, the Fairchild managers (including Noyce and other key leaders from Palo Alto), who formed Intel in 1968 as a new venture, sought to organize their new firm to streamline the flow of technology from R&D to product application in the market.

Their basic idea was to replace bimodal organization of technology development (R&D to production) with a three-step waterfall structure. Two or more small steps replaced the single large step between the laboratory and the manufacturing floor. Since each successive organization faced progressively larger-scale production goals, they consisted of people who could talk on the same level with personnel in adjacent organizations. Information tended to flow far more freely, both up and down the chain. Transfers of personnel between the various departments were frequent, and were encouraged when processes or products were to be moved from one department to another.

Intel's organizational structure evolved over the years from 1969 to the present, and is continuing to change as the business expands. In addition, the nature of the technology shifted to production of volume memory manufacturing and to microprocessors and computer products. Intel continues to modify its technological organization to adapt to the changes in production technology and investment necessary to continue progress in the semiconductor field.

The Fairchild/Intel example illustrates a continuity of experimentation with the technological structure of the companies. The same principles could apply to nontechnical functions, but the barriers shown here seem more common between departments dealing with technological matters than between other departments such as personnel or finance. "Not-invented-here" thinking, often noted as a barrier to technological cooperation between firms, seems a hindrance to internal cooperation as well.

CHALLENGE NINE: MANAGING QUALITY

Product quality is a traditional goal for virtually every manufacturing and service business. Few companies deliberately set out to produce products that are inferior to their competitors' goods. Yet, until a decade ago, many American companies generally felt that their product quality was "good enough"—sufficient to compete in domestic and world markets. Improved product quality, it was reasoned, would cost more, reducing product competitiveness.

Product and service quality is now receiving renewed attention. Lessons learned from Japanese successes in the automobile, camera, and consumer electronics industries clearly indicate the competitive advantages of high quality in customer acceptance and warranty costs. As a result, many U.S. firms have stressed quality improvement in production operations, using intensive testing, inspection, and reduction of equipment and operator errors. Many of these recent attempts echo quality efforts of the 1960s, such as the Zero Defects Program, that arose from the needs of the space program. Most of them are limited in their effectiveness.

The perception of quality as primarily a production add-on—as evidenced in product testing and inspection programs—misses a fundamental point. Product and service quality is *not* just something that can be added at the conclusion of production. Outgoing inspection does not compensate for errors, detectable or not, that occur during manufacturing. The cost of product rejected during production inspection can be a significant drag on attempts to reduce manufacturing costs. Time lost and the defective product built while waiting for results of outgoing product tests to detect production process problems are unacceptable. Quality assurance cannot simply be delegated to a supervisory quality department. As such, quality is a crucial aspect of product- and process-improvement commercialization.

The works of W. Edwards Deming,[6] Joseph M. Juran,[7] and others have related improvements in production operations to statistical process experimentation, characterization, and control. In the "new" production ideal, process control replaces product control. Once processes are characterized, corrective actions respond to leading indicators of process problems *before* bad product is produced. Scrap due to out-of-tolerance processes is eliminated, and the wait for results of final product tests to determine corrective actions is gone. Improvements in individual process step control are clearly reflected in significant improvements in final product quality and reliability. In addition, consistency and corrective response to process problems as they occur, instead of after the fact, can significantly reduce manufacturing costs. The philosophy of building quality into the product through intrinsic process control works and has been demonstrated over and over in many industries and companies.

True product and service quality, however, goes well beyond production process control. It must be inherent in product and process design, the marriage of product and process, and production implementation. Quality affects more than the products produced; it significantly affects the economics of production, since design for manufacturing matches process control capabilities to the necessary product and service tolerances and seeks to minimize the manufacturing costs by minimizing the number of parts and simplifying manufacturing operations. The result is inherently lower input costs and still higher production yields. The standard of competitiveness for quality has undergone a profound change. The standard is no longer a fixed goal but a continuous process.

A new generation of quality programs, intended to produce a permanent change in company attitudes, is arising. At Xerox it is called "Leadership Through Quality"; at Intel it is called the "Total Quality Program"; and at Hewlett-Packard, "Total Quality Control." AT&T has instituted an extensive, company-wide quality improvement cycle. Other firms have referred to the change as "Total Quality Management." These programs are sustained efforts led by company management that has become inspired with the prospect of converting the entire company to a continuous improvement quality culture. One example is the Six Sigma program at Motorola.

Motorola's leaders became concerned in the late 1970s when they compared the quality of their products with that of comparable Japanese products. The company initiated a program to improve product quality by a factor of five in five years. When they discovered that this initial goal was met in three years instead of five, they began to wonder how far quality improvement could be pushed—they asked what the concept of "zero defects" really means. Their answer, based on a simplified statistical model of the manufacturing process, is a program called "Six Sigma." It has become a guiding principle throughout the company.

Motorola reasoned that a typical manufacturing process consists of 1,200 individual, independent steps. If the statistical distribution of the results of each of these steps is described by a normal (Gaussian) distribution of standard deviation sigma (σ), the accumulated action of the individual process steps on overall process quality can be modeled. If the process tolerance window for each step is $\pm 3\sigma$ (considered good in many production situations), 99.73% of product produced at that step will be good. The fallout rate is therefore 2,700 parts per million (ppm) for that particular step. That sounds pretty good, except that the accumulated result of 1,200 manufacturing steps, each with $\pm 3\sigma$ tolerance, is 3,240,000 errors per 1,000,000 units produced—an average of 3.24 defects per unit.

Using this simplified model, Motorola went on to calculate that $\pm 4\sigma$ tolerances resulted in 75,600 ppm final quality, $\pm 5\sigma$ in 684 parts per million, and $\pm 6\sigma$ in 2.4 parts per million. Motorola settled on the 6σ tolerance limit as its initial approximation for "zero defects." With $\pm 6\sigma$ tolerances, each process step has to produce good product 99.9999998% of the time—the error rate is 2 parts per billion.

Motorola began routinely rating its production line performance in terms of sigma. With the "sigma" figure of merit as an overall guide, manufacturing people began to uncover and solve individual process step problems, one at a time, in order of their impact on overall line results. Soon the effort spread to product and process design, as the contribution of those activities became apparent. The company next set out to apply the Six Sigma philosophy to company operations outside of manufacturing. They began to set comparable goals and to rate salesmen, staff, and even

the chief executive's office in terms of sigma performance measures. The company has insisted that its
suppliers undertake a similar approach to quality,
reasoning that to have a truly high-quality company,
Motorola must involve everyone concerned with its
operations.

Initially, none of Motorola's activities came any-
where near 6σ performance, but the company began to
act as if it could reach that goal. It has made substantial progress. The resultant effect on quality was recognized in 1988, when Motorola was named the first
corporate winner of the U.S. government's Malcolm
Baldrige National Quality Award. The Six Sigma effort continues as Motorola executives quietly wonder
what the next goal will be after six sigma.

To be effective, such a quality concern must be a perpetual
focus within the company. The new concept of pervasive
quality cannot be implemented through periodic efforts. A
"program of the month" lacks the sustained, determined attention needed for continuous improvement. Sporadic approaches and hyperbole build distrust for such programs
among employees, many of whom are likely to sap well-
intentioned efforts with a "this too shall pass" attitude. A
quality improvement program must be more than a collection of new year's resolutions. Good intentions are not
enough: there must be means to track improvements that
relate to overall company performance. An additional danger in formal quality programs is that, in time, they will
develop into a caricature of themselves. Programs that become stale tend to develop a life of their own, out of step with
original intentions.

Leaders of commercialization activities must incorporate
continuous quality improvement throughout their efforts
and, clearly, quality should be a central concern in commercializing new products. Quality assurance efforts cannot be
limited to production activities; they must pervade all as-

pects of technology selection and development, design, process, production, and marketing. A high-quality product can be reliably produced only by a process whose capabilities and control match the product design; attributes of product quality must match customer expectations for product performance and durability.

Indeed, leading firms have come to realize that quality should be a basis for all company operations. The idea of total quality is that every activity must be conducted with the highest quality possible and that efforts to improve quality must preoccupy every employee, partner, and supplier. The decisions of the chief executive officer, order entry clerks, human relations people, the traffic and shipping group, the sales and marketing force, and the finance, legal, and accounting departments should follow the same quality process criteria and scrutiny as engineering and manufacturing activities. Each affects the company's ability to meet customer needs and expectations and thus affects the competitiveness of the firm.

The literature on the "how to" of total quality improvement is vast and growing rapidly,[8] as are scholarly treatises on the meaning of quality[9] and collections of examples of good quality processes, products, and services.[10] The scope and complexity of what can only be called the quality movement in the United States is enormous, and the intent here is to draw attention to its importance for successful innovation.

CHALLENGE TEN:
KNOWING WHEN AND HOW TO QUIT

Perhaps the most difficult commercialization decision for managers is to halt a development project. All the organizational and emotional inertia that can be a barrier to starting a new effort can be more of an impediment to stopping. There are always enticing reasons to stay with an effort, even well after its initial promise has faded. The weight of investments already made, the feeling that success is just around the corner, and reluctance to admit that an effort has failed to achieve its promise all argue for continuation. Yet competitive market developments, inability to achieve key timing or performance milestones, or the prospect of cost increases out of line with expected income all indicate the need for drastic action. Many of these factors are indicated by project progress tools such as time-to-break-even analysis.

Commercialization always involves some element of risk, so it should not be surprising that some product, process, and service developments do not reach fruition. The greatest opportunity for failure in commercialization management lies not in discontinuing an activity when it is clear that it is not going to produce a distinctive product or manufacturing capability in a timely manner, but in sinking more resources into the effort after its promise has faded.

The logic of sunk costs is simple—expenses incurred yesterday do not matter to today's actions; marginal dollars should be spent only if there is a reasonable prospect of earning the dollar back plus an acceptable return. Organizations, however, are not often amenable to such simple logic. Large amounts of money and individuals' careers become "invested" in particular developments, product lines, or process improvements. It is often remarkably difficult to stop doing something—Hughes's Spruce Goose airplane and AT&T's Picturephone® projects are examples of dogged determination to proceed long after the promise of success had dwindled.

Timing is a particularly important consideration in deciding whether or not to continue with a commercialization effort. Many commercialization activities have "windows of opportunity" in time. After the window closes (marked perhaps by the market entry of a given number of competitors), the opportunity is lost. In such an instance, project continuation according to the original plan is questionable, and a failure to exit can be very costly.

The ability of enthusiasm and a vision to overwhelm good sense, to stop a company or an investor from walking away from a bad idea, is illustrated by the history of an American icon—the Pony Express. In the 1830s and 1840s the emergence of railroad service bred the proliferation of express mail and package companies. These private entities worked well in local areas, but the vast distances of the North American continent defeated them. In the 1840s mail service between Boston and San Francisco took a month only if everything went well. Some mail traveled by ship to the isthmus of Panama, overland to the Pacific, and then by ship again to San Francisco. At the same time, the telegraph was being developed and introduced, with the first service provided between Washington and Baltimore in 1844 and with more than 23,000 miles of lines among 500 cities and villages (in the eastern United States) by 1852.

The competition among express companies was fierce. A well-known express entrepreneur, William Russell, won a contract to deliver mail between New York and San Francisco in thirteen days if it was sent to St. Joseph, Missouri, by rail and nine days if the message was telegraphed to St. Joseph from New York. His Pony Express service began in April 1860—the same year Congress passed and President James Buchanan signed the Pacific Telegraph Act to link West Coast and East Coast telegraph systems.

The Pony Express project was started despite the knowledge that the transcontinental telegraph was imminent. The Pony Express network cost $100,000 to set up and was an immediate public relations success. Mark Twain, in his book Roughing It, *described the enthusiastic crowds that would gather to watch and cheer the riders as they galloped through a town. But enthusiasm wasn't enough. By the end of 1860, Russell had lost $1 million, and prospects were not good. The service ended in October of 1861, the same month that transcontinental telegraph service was established. Transcon-*

tinental rail service was established eight years later, making the express transport of packages as well as messages possible.[11]

Timely management decisions to discontinue unproductive projects to conserve resources for other, more productive activities are a necessary part of the commercialization process. As unpleasant as these decisions are, they are the only way of coping with the downside of risky commercialization ventures. The decision to stop is almost always unpleasant, but sometimes necessary.

5

The Competitive Advantage of the Firm

On Technology, Strategy, and Style

The general who wins a battle makes many calculations in his temple before the battle is fought. The general who loses a battle makes but few calculations beforehand. Thus do many calculations lead to victory, and a few calculations to defeat; how much more no calculations at all! It is by attention to this point that I can foresee who is likely to win or lose.

SUN TZU, *The Art of War*

The scope and scale of today's technology are sufficiently large that no production manager, technologist, or laboratory of technologists can possibly work with or even know about it all. Effective use of technology requires a business plan that recognizes the full range of applicable technologies and identifies how a particular technological capability can make possible products or processes that are useful to the company. Management must distinguish between armchair prognostication about the potential of this or that technology and the real potential of something available for constructive use. This is *not* an easy task. A recent book by Steven P. Schnaars is an excellent and humbling catalog of technological/business forecasting errors of the last several decades.[1]

Deciding that a particular technology will be useful, once developed, is largely a result of technological and business imagination, combined (when the development is far enough along that there is real information) with analysis of business economics and markets. The mechanisms by which technology is developed, acquired, or applied are crucial but are less important than a clear sense of purpose in the pursuit of the goal. Management must provide a constancy of purpose that can allow the search for, selection, and development of technologies based on a clear perception of business needs and opportunities. Rosabeth Moss Kanter describes it as the key to adopting technology:

> [C]orporate strategy is clearly a key to whether or not organizations are good at adopting and using new technology. Technology will be acceptable if it is seen as part of the competitive advantage of the firm and, therefore, will get resources and attention. Effective adoption and use of technological innovation requires a strategic decision that this innovation should get resources allocated to it, resources necessary to exploit its potential. For product and technical process innovations, and even for some organizational innovations, the greatest financial requirements begin after the model has been developed. Thus, the nature of the strategic decision process and how top management is linked to the innovation project is another critical structural element in an innovation's success or failure.[2]

Management also has the obligation to know and understand what they are managing. There is no substitute for the energy and focus that come from an organizational commitment to winning—to creating and keeping a comparative advantage through superior quality, function, price, or other delivered characteristics. The essence of durable success in profiting from innovation is a continual, aggressive, organization-wide focus on the fundamental (sometimes technological) aspects of business. Bill Boeing provided this focus for the company he founded when he said, "Let no advance in flying pass us by." He did not say, "let no opportunity to make a buck pass us by" or "let no opportunity to diversify pass us by."

Developing and effectively using technology requires a type of knowledge, patience, and intensity that may differ from other business attributes. This is as true for insurance companies learning to use global telecommunications as it is for the most R&D-intensive bioengineering firms. Environments where emphasis is on liquidity of investments—on short-term returns—are especially challenging to technical managers, as it is often simply not possible to make quick-return investments in new products, processes, and services. The balancing return to a long-term risk, of course, is that new technologies can create entirely new markets or firmly consolidate market leadership positions. The risk to the organization (and often to the jobs of leaders in the organization) arises because many technologies do fail as business bases, and it is difficult to assess, even well into the development process, which will be winners, which losers. Unfortunately, current strategy-formulation practices in many companies do not provide the kind of insight needed for long-term risk taking.

The popularity of planning in the past 15 to 20 years has made formal strategy development a ritual in most firms' annual business cycle. All too often, in medium-size to large companies, management delegates formulation of the strategy to a planning staff whose success is measured by the gross weight of planning documents produced or by adherence to a rigid planning process. In such an environment where form triumphs over content, and where senior management consummates its role in an annual day-long review of an encyclopedic "plan," it is no wonder that operations diverge from the plan.

Effective planning—strategy development—and implementation fuse market insight, competitor assessments, technology choice, production and marketing plans, and financial goals. As such, strategy plays a crucial role in commercialization. Much has been written and taught about developing plans, strategy design, and case studies of "good" and "bad" strategies. For commercialization purposes, a strategy must clearly set forth what a product (or process) is, how it is to be realized, its place in the market, its introduction timing, and how a company can make money from a new technology and perhaps from similar future developments. Although strategies and plans can often be wide of the mark, the value of the forecast and analysis is the focus they provide.

To the manager, much of the value of strategy formulation lies in personally drawing the major aspects of business operations together in a formal thinking process. The objective of the process is integration of the principal business activities in a set of working guidelines that are useful in the day-to-day business context. The purpose of the strategy is not limited to technology development, production implementation, or market actions—the result must be the integration of these and more into a successful business operation. This means that no successful commercialization plan exists separate from the general business plan and that a thorough understanding of customer needs and market issues—also understanding the most effective technological tools available to design and produce successful products—is indispensable. If a corporate strategy depends on new technology, managers should, early in the planning process, identify the type of commercialization processes (technology-driven, market-driven, product- and process-driven, or end game) at work in a given product or process realization. This understanding can help identify a realistic time for execution, likely areas of risk, organizational alternatives, appropriate tools for monitoring progress, and potential management challenges.

Edwin Mansfield and his colleagues at the University of Pennsylvania brought home the importance of realistic expectations and plans through their work in the pharmaceutical industry. They explored the ratios of actual to expected cost and time in bringing a new product to market. In an ethical drug firm, the ratio of actual-to-expected cost was 1.78 and actual-to-expected time was 1.61. In a proprietary drug firm, the comparable ratios were 2.11 (cost) and 2.95 (time).[3] If these firms typify U.S. corporations, there is obviously a widespread failure to assess or understand the time and resources necessary to bring products to market. These considerations can help frame the issues to be addressed by a realistic strategy. Similar examples in the aerospace industry reveal a basic conflict between innovation and accurate cost and schedule forecasting. *Any significant innovation in technology or mission involves risks such that cost and schedule cannot be precisely known at the start.* Conversely, if it is possible to forecast cost and schedule precisely, the project may well be obsolete.

Also, while it seems obvious that any strategy and planning process must lead to actions that will most likely produce the desired results, this is often not true in practice. Gaps can develop between formal plans and execution, and these differences go unseen if strategy formulation is an isolated exercise or only loosely coupled to other activities of the enterprise. Figure 5–1 is a stylized illustration of actual and planned sales for one short-cycle business over many years. Note that although the sales goals for each year rose steeply according to the sum of the plans of the various parts of the business, the actual sales curve slowly undulated, with little long-term increase. Clearly the actual results deviated substantially from the long-range plan. This illustrates a chronic problem that can appear in new product introduction, manufacturing, or any other major part of an enterprise. The gap between planned and actual results should not repeat in such a consistent manner.

In this example, annual planning was an isolated event, independent of previous strategies and plans. Each year's blueprint for the future looked forward, and did not consider results of past strategies. When the large disparity between past plans and actual results was noted, the company chose

Figure 5–1 Forecasts and Results: The "Hockey Stick" Effect in Planning and Managing

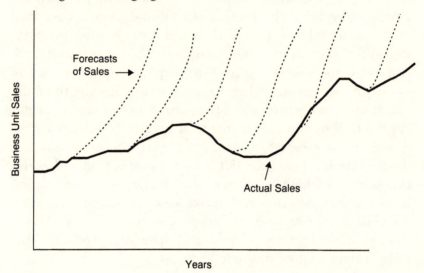

to begin each successive planning discussion with a complete review of previous objectives and results, and sought feedback to find reasons why the two did not agree. Lessons learned were used to correct subsequent strategies.

Effective feedback in the planning process allows strategic planning to be flexible and to include unanticipated or creative ideas or events that characterize the disordered environment of many businesses. Effective business strategies must allow sufficient slack to adjust to reasonable changes and allow the kind of exploratory activity that can lead to new opportunities for the business.

Finally, the personal involvement by senior management in commercialization activities is characteristic of companies with successful commercialization records, as illustrated by remarks by Henry Kressel, managing director, Warburg, Pincus Ventures.

In companies where the CEO is not cognizant of the industry status *in detail* the tendency is to delegate key responsibility for the future of the business without really understanding that they have done so. Therefore, the process of new product investment, more often than not, becomes a "political process" driven by the ambitions of individuals rather than the concern for the long-term welfare of the corporation. The result is chaotic product planning and panic-driven reaction to market developments which come as surprises to uninformed managers.[4]

The trick is to moderate involvement: stay in close touch with projects and impending problems, but do not dominate the activity so that the subordinate leaders lose their incentive to make management decisions.

Senior leadership must provide direction, nurture commercialization efforts, and instill a winning attitude in an organization. Technological leadership requires a passion for the technological and business aspects of a company, not a detached, analytical approach to leading. Merely presiding over autonomous business units or subordinates does not provide the coordination and focus that should be a part of any business. Simply coping with the status quo is an invitation to more aggressive competitors to seize leadership in attractive products and markets.

A leader's active involvement in the company's commercialization efforts shows dedication to the continuing health of the business. A leader's presence, encouragement, and participation is crucial to the morale of the workers. It also helps a leader understand project progress and remove obstacles as they arise. Managers who rely on monthly reviews as their main window on their operations lose contact with the process and can react only after problems become serious.

Time spent working with development activities is so important that it should be integrated into every leader's calendar. Otherwise, more immediate activities will divert attention from efforts to secure the future of the business. Leadership's role is to be an agent of change for the business, and this requires effort, energy, and patience.

6

Final Thoughts

Everything that can be invented has been invented.

CHARLES H. DUELL, Commissioner of the U.S. Office of Patents, urging
President William McKinley to abolish the patent office in 1899

While many aspects of business practice would seem to have changed dramatically in the last hundred years, much clearly remains unchanged except by technological advance. Stock markets still reveal prices, but the volume of transactions—180 million shares on a typical day at the New York Stock Exchange—would be impossible without sophisticated communications and computers. Consumers still buy food, clothing, toys, and health care, but the specifics have changed. Products and services are now designed, produced, delivered, and sold worldwide using technology-based systems not imaginable fifty years ago. Advances in transportation and innovations in food handling make inexpensive fresh food available nationwide in grocery stores, in fast food restaurants, and in microwavable pouches for home use throughout the year.

Industrial technological innovation has altered not only products but also the companies that make and deliver those products. A global bank or manufacturing concern today has little in common, organizationally, with its predecessor of one hundred years ago. Business structures develop over time in a way that is consistent with the requirements of competition and the opportunities of technological advance. The complexity, timing, and overlapping nature of technological changes are subtle and important elements of almost any business environment.

Revolutionary technological advances—those announced with great fanfare on the pages of popular journals—usually have long gestation periods between the original invention or discovery and its application in products and services. As Table 6–1 shows, many important inventions can take a long time to become commercially viable products or services. Sometimes, technology itself is the pacing factor as problems of application, manufacture, or design are worked out. In other cases, the pacing factors in the commercialization of a new product or service are undeveloped supporting or complementary technologies, or necessary changes in structure of the businesses or market handling the product or service. In extreme cases, success of a revolutionary technology may have to wait for infrastructure development.

Table 6–1 Duration of the Innovative Process of Ten Innovations of High Social Impact

Innovation	Year of First Conception	Year of First Realization	Duration (Years)
Heart pacemaker	1928	1960	32
Hybrid corn	1908	1933	25
Hybrid small grains	1937	1956	19
Green revolution wheat	1950	1966	16
Electrophotography	1937	1959	22
Input-output economic analysis	1936	1964	28
Organophosphorus insecticides	1934	1947	13
Oral contraceptive	1951	1960	9
Magnetic ferrites	1933	1955	22
Video tape recorder	1950	1956	6
Average Duration			19.2

SOURCE: *Science, Technology, and Innovation.* Prepared for NSF by Battelle Columbus Laboratories (Columbus, Ohio), Contract NSF-C 667, February 1973, p. 9.

Evolutionary technological change in a product or service happens much more quickly but still may be slower than shifts in other business operations simply because of the character of technological change. Each business has characteristic cycle times, and the period of technological change must translate directly into the temporal requirements for successful technological operations. For example, a 24-month program and cost-definition phase preceded the 49-month activity from production go-ahead to first delivery of the first Boeing 767, as illustrated by Figure 6–1. There was a similarly long time—10 years—for development and deployment of the first transatlantic, submarine fiber-optic cable. In many industries, ability to compete in the long run depends on rapid, error-free improvement of processes and products. A successful firm must continually beat its competitors to the market with technological improvements to reach and sustain a winning position.

Commercialization of product, process, and service innovations is bound to be a complex process. By its very nature,

Figure 6–1 Typical Production Program: Boeing 767 Program Phases

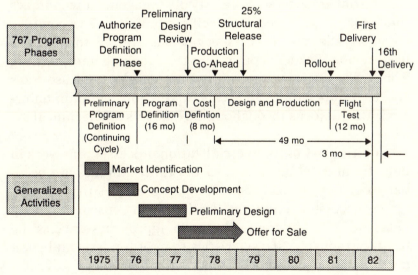

SOURCE: The Boeing Company.

commercialization of technologies breeds confusion as a result of both unforeseeable market and competitive developments, and the chaos that accompanies the invention, development, and marketing processes within a firm. As a basis for action in this complex environment, a manager needs to develop several important skills:

- Awareness of the pervasive and complex nature of technological change
- Sensitivity to patterns of technological, market, and industrial development
- Appreciation for how technological change creates business opportunities
- Imagination to envision how available or potentially available technology can yield new products for future markets
- Appreciation that most new technology-based business ideas fail in the marketplace
- Ability to recognize how lessons learned in everyday experience might contribute to the business future

Such attributes constitute a prepared mind, the first step toward success. They prepare a manager to consider and select from among a wide variety of management techniques that must be adapted to specific situations. The complex commercialization process is not susceptible to a single, fixed recipe. Leaders committed to managing and profiting from technological innovation must develop and use tools and techniques that can create, drive, and maintain an organizational focus throughout the business and technical cycle.

A multiplicity of commercialization processes is at work in industry and, while certain successful techniques are peculiar to given business sectors, many practices that characterize successful commercialization seem consistent among industries. The differences between approaches are less the result of industry characteristics than of fundamental commercialization drivers—revolutionary technology advance, new market opportunity, product or process improvement,

or decisions confronting maturing businesses. Each type of
process has its own risk factors, rate of progress, organizational precepts, and analytic tools for decision making. In
view of this, an important management skill lies in recognizing when each type of process is at work, understanding
its nature and applying appropriate measures to encourage
success.

The taxonomy of commercialization processes presented
in this book is illustrated in terms and with examples that
are intended to develop clear distinctions among types of
commercialization challenges. As discussed in this book, four
types of commercialization challenges occur during early,
middle, and late stages in the life of a commercial technology:

- Both *technology-driven* and *market-driven* commercialization challenges occur early in the life of a new commercial technology, when value lies in the search for
  applications and means, and when benefits come from
  being early to market with the right technology.
- *Product- and process-improvement* commercialization
  challenges occur later, when value comes from executing
  product, process, quality, or service improvements
  sooner than others do.
- The challenges of the *end game* occur still later, when
  value comes from correctly managing technological maturity.

In many cases, the actual situation a manager faces will not
be as clear as those presented in this book, and insight and
leadership and skill will be necessary to determine the true
nature of challenge. In most cases, however, understanding
the nature of the four types of commercialization process can
provide a critical edge in selecting the correct measures to
prosecute a given project.

In addition to understanding and adapting management
methods to the nature of specific projects encountered, commercialization leaders face a number of common challenges
in creating an environment where commercialization can

flourish. The need to manage the various project goals, yet allow for sufficient flexibility to encourage creativity and technological communication, is at the heart of the corporate innovative environment. Each of the challenges spelled out in the chapter on organization and management, including nurturing of champions, technical information transfer, organization structures, and joint development management, is a part of maintaining a healthy climate for commercialization of technical innovations.

All this means that successful commercialization leaders must ceaselessly seek to understand the true nature of the technology, markets, and commercialization activities. Managing technological innovation is not often a cold-blooded matter. Many of the best managers of commercialization activities love the product or service they provide, are obsessive about customer satisfaction, and can infect others with the burning desire to make a meaningful contribution to design, development, production, and delivery of a product or service. Managing profiting from innovation can rarely be done at arm's length.

Finally, commercialization success is not a single event—it is the result of a series of triumphs and failures, each providing an entry point to the challenge of the next. Dealing effectively with this series of challenges requires that business leaders, just like military leaders, be able to separate the true nature of the contest from the smoke and dust that obscure the situation. Leaders must be sufficiently aware of activities under way and of forces at work in the market that they can understand the impact of their actions.

Notes

Preface and Acknowledgments

1. Panel on Invention and Innovation, U.S. Department of Commerce, *Technological Innovation: Its Environment and Management* (Washington, D.C.: Government Printing Office, 1967), p. 56.

Chapter 1. Why This Book?

1. R. Reich, *The Resurgent Liberal* (New York: Vintage, 1989), pp. 7–8.

Chapter 2. The Prepared Mind: Understanding Technological Innovation in Industry

1. D. Owen, "Copies in Seconds." *The Atlantic*, February 1986, p. 65. Owen admits that eleventy zillion is a made up statistic and reports, but questions as too low, the Xerox public-relations department estimate of 522 billion copies made in 1985. © 1986 by David Owen, reprinted from *The Atlantic*.
2. N. Rosenberg, *Inside the Black Box: Technology and Economics* (New York: Cambridge University Press, 1982).
3. A. D. Chandler, Jr., *The Visible Hand* (Cambridge, Mass.: The Belknap Press of Harvard University Press, 1977); and *Scale and Scope: The Dynamics of Industrial Capitalism* (Cambridge, Mass.: The Belknap Press of Harvard University Press, 1990).
4. See W. J. Abernathy and J. M. Utterback, "Patterns of Industrial Innovation," *Technology Review*, June–July 1978, pp. 40–47; G. Dosi, *Technical Change and Industrial Transformation* (New York: St. Martin's Press, 1984); J. C. Fisher and R. H. Pry, "A Simple Substitution Model of Technological Change," *Technological Forecasting and Social Change*, Vol. 3, 1971, pp. 75–78; R. N. Foster, "Boosting the Payoff from R&D," *Research Management*, January 1982, pp. 22–27; R. N. Foster, *Innovation: The Attacker's Advantage* (New York: Summit Books, 1986); R. E. Gomory, "From the 'Ladder of Science' to the Product Development Cycle," *Harvard Business Review*,

November–December 1989, pp. 99–105; R. R. Nelson and S. G. Winter, *An Evolutionary Theory of Economic Change* (Cambridge, Mass.: The Belknap Press of Harvard University Press, 1982); *Technology in Society*, Special Issue on Technology in the Modern Corporation—A Strategic Perspective, Vol. 7, No. 2/3, 1985; and M. L. Tushman and W. L. Moore, *Readings in the Management of Innovation* (New York: Ballinger Publishing Co., 1982).

5. After P. R. Nayak and J. M. Ketteringham, *Breakthroughs!* (New York: Rawson Associates, 1986).

6. Robert Lucky, Executive Director of the Research Communications Sciences Division, AT&T Bell Laboratories, paper presented at the National Academy of Engineering Symposium on Engineering as a Social Enterprise, Washington, D.C., October 3, 1990.

7. Based on F. A. Fellows and D. N. Frey, "Pictures and Parts: Delivering an Automated Automotive Parts Catalog," in *Managing Innovation: Cases from the Services Industries* (Washington, D.C.: National Academy Press, 1988).

8. F. R. Bacon, Jr., and T. W. Butler, Jr., *Planned Innovation*, Institute of Science and Technology, The University of Michigan, Ann Arbor, 1981.

9. Gomory, "From the 'Ladder of Science,' " p. 102.

10. Further reading on these topics includes G. E. Taguchi and T. Hsiang, *Quality Engineering in Production Systems* (New York: McGraw-Hill, 1989); Gomory, "When Technology Drives Competition"; D. A. Garvin "What Does 'Product Quality' Really Mean?" *Sloan Management Review*, Fall 1984, pp. 25–43; and R. Jaikumar, "Postindustrial manufacturing," *Harvard Business Review*, November–December 1986, pp. 69–76.

11. L. Seifert, "Design and Analysis of Integrated Electronics Manufacturing Systems," in *Design and Analysis of Integrated Manufacturing Systems* (Washington, D.C.: National Academy Press, 1988), pp. 12–33.

12. After R. Jaikumar, "From Filing and Fitting to Flexible Manufacturing: A Study in the Evolution of Process Control," Harvard Business School Working Paper Series #88045, 1988–89.

13. The Boston Consulting Group, *Perspectives #66—The Product Portfolio* (Boston: Boston Consulting Group, 1970).

14. Not all of the "stiffness" in the system is a function of market forces. For example, it has been argued that product liability concerns can be a barrier to product upgrading; corporations

can be concerned that upgrading a product signals a deficiency in the prior design and can open the door to legal action on product liability grounds.

Chapter 3. Management Tools and Techniques

1. Robert Frosch, Vice President R&D, General Motors Corporation, paper presented at the National Academy of Engineering Symposium on World Technologies and National Sovereignty, Washington, D.C., February 13–14, 1986.

2. Donald Frey, Professor of Industrial Engineering and Management Sciences, Northwestern University, and former Chairman and CEO, Bell & Howell Company, paper presented at the National Academy of Engineering Symposium on the Role of Universities in National Economic Development, Washington, D.C., December 7, 1990.

3. See J. R. Dixon, A. J. Nanni, and T. E. Vollmann, *The New Performance Challenge: Measuring Operations for World-Class Competition* (Homewood, Ill.: Dow Jones-Irwin, 1990); H. T. Johnson and R. S. Kaplan, *Relevance Lost: The Rise and Fall of Management Accounting* (Cambridge, Mass.: Harvard Business School Press, 1987); and R. S. Kaplan, ed., *Measures for Manufacturing Excellence* (Boston: Harvard Business School Press, 1990).

4. Based on D. K. Smith and R. C. Alexander, *Fumbling the Future* (New York: William Morrow, 1988).

5. A. D. Chandler, Jr., *Scale and Scope: The Dynamics of Industrial Capitalism* (Cambridge, Mass.: The Belknap Press of Harvard University Press, 1990).

6. C. K. Prahalad and G. Hamel, "The Core Competence of the Corporation," *Harvard Business Review*, May–June 1990, pp. 79–91.

7. L. Krogh, J. Prager, D. Sorensen, and J. Tomlinson, "How 3M Evaluates Its R&D Programs," *Research and Technology Management*, November/December 1988, pp. 10–14.

8. Robert Charpie, former chairman, Cabot Corporation, remarks presented during National Academy of Engineering Workshop on Profiting from Innovation, Woods Hole, Mass., August 1988.

9. For further information see F. R. Bacon, Jr., and T. W. Butler, Jr., *Planned Innovation*, Institute of Science and Technology, The University of Michigan, Ann Arbor, 1981.

10. John Hesselberth, E. I. du Pont de Nemours and Company,

remarks presented during the National Academy of Engineering Workshop on Profiting from Innovation, Woods Hole, Mass., August 1988.

11. National Society of Professional Engineers, *Engineering Stages of New Product Development* (Alexandria, Va.: National Society of Professional Engineers, 1990).

12. Ibid., pp. 16–23. Reprinted by permission of the National Society of Professional Engineers.

13. Also called a return map; see C. H. House and R. L. Price, "The Return Map: Tracking Product Teams," *Harvard Business Review*, January–February 1991, pp. 92–100.

14. H. Barry Bebb, Vice President for Systems Architecture, Xerox Corporation, paper presented during technical session of the National Academy of Engineering annual meeting, Washington, D.C., October 14, 1988. Xerox continued to vigorously pursue competitive benchmarking as a major element of its quality process and achieved enormous improvements (and, in 1989, received the Malcolm Baldrige National Quality Award).

15. For further information about benchmarking practice and theory see R. C. Camp, *Benchmarking: The Search for Industry Best Practices that Lead to Superior Performance* (Milwaukee, Wis.: ASQC Quality Press, 1989).

16. The Boston Consulting Group, *Perspectives on Experience* (Boston: Boston Consulting Group, 1969); R. Nanda and G. Alder, *Learning Curves: Theory and Application* (Norcross, Ga.: Industrial Engineering and Management Press of the Institute of Industrial Engineers, 1982); L. E. Yelle, "The Learning Curve: Historical Review and Comprehensive Survey," *Decision Sciences*, Vol. 10, 1979, pp. 302–328; and S. L. Young, "Misapplications of Learning Curve Concept," *Journal of Industrial Engineering*, August 1966, pp. 410–415.

17. C. H. Willyard and C. W. McClees, "Motorola's Technology Roadmap Process," *Research Management*, September–October 1987, pp. 13–19.

18. D. J. Teece, "Capturing Value from Technological Innovation: Integration, Strategic Partnering, and Licensing Decisions," in *Technology and Global Industry*, B. Guile and H. Brooks, eds. (Washington, D.C.: National Academy Press, 1987), pp. 65–95.

19. T. Modis and A. Debecker, "Innovation in the Computer Indus-

try," *Technological Forecasting and Social Change*, Vol. 33, 1988, pp. 267–278.

Chapter 4. A New Order of Things: Organization and Management of Commercialization Activities

1. R. M. Kanter, "Improving the Acceptance and Use of Technology: Organizational and Interorganizational Challenge," in *Designing for Technological Change: People in the Process* (Washington, D.C.: National Academy Press, 1991).

2. J. B. Quinn, "Innovation and Corporate Strategy: Managed Chaos," *Technology in Society*, Vol. 7, No. 2/3, 1985, pp. 263–279.

3. T. J. Allen, *Managing the Flow of Technology: Technology Transfer and the Dissemination of Technological Information within the R&D Organization* (Cambridge, Mass.: MIT Press, 1977).

4. *Directory of Engineering Societies and Related Organizations* (Washington, D.C.: American Association of Engineering Societies, 1989).

5. Based on a presentation by Timothy S. Killen, manager, Engineering and Construction Technologies, Bechtel National, Inc. at National Academy of Engineering Workshop on Profiting from Innovation, Woods Hole, Mass., August 1988.

6. W. E. Deming, *Quality, Productivity, and Competitive Position* (Cambridge, Mass.: MIT Center for Advanced Engineering Study, 1982); and W. E. Deming, *Out of the Crisis* (Cambridge, Mass.: MIT Center for Advanced Engineering Study, 1986).

7. J. M. Juran and F. M. Gryna, *Quality Planning and Analysis* (New York: McGraw-Hill, 1980).

8. For example, see M. Imai, *Kaizen* (New York: McGraw-Hill, 1986); and W. W. Scherkenbach, *The Deming Route to Quality and Productivity: Road Maps and Roadblocks* (George Washington University, Washington, D.C.: Cee Press Books, 1988).

9. D. A. Garvin, "What Does 'Product Quality' Really Mean?" *Sloan Management Review*, Fall 1984, pp. 25–43; and D. A. Garvin, *Managing Quality: The Strategic and Competitive Edge* (New York: The Free Press, 1988).

10. J. W. Spechler, *When America Does It Right* (Norcross, Ga.: Industrial Engineering and Management Press, 1988).

11. Based on R. Sobel and D. Sicilia, *The Entrepreneurs: An American Adventure* (Boston: Houghton Mifflin, 1986).

Chapter 5. The Competitive Advantage of the Firm: On Technology, Strategy, and Style

1. S. P. Schnaars, *Megamistakes: Forecasting and the Myth of Rapid Technological Change* (New York: The Free Press, 1989).

2. R. M. Kanter, "Improving the Acceptance and Use of Technology: Organizational and Interorganizational Challenge," in *Designing for Technological Change: People in the Process* (Washington, D.C.: National Academy Press, 1991).

3. Edwin Mansfield, et al., *Research and Innovation in the Modern Corporation* (New York: W. W. Norton, 1971), p. 211.

4. Henry Kressel, Managing Director, Warburg, Pincus Ventures, Inc., private communication, January 7, 1990.

Study Committee on Profiting from Innovation

WILLIAM G. HOWARD, JR., is a Senior Fellow at the National Academy of Engineering, where he was elected a member in 1985. Howard received the Senior Fellow appointment following a career at Motorola, Inc., where he began as manager of linear integrated circuits research and later served as senior vice president and corporate director of research and development. Howard received his Ph.D. degree from the University of California, Berkeley, and M.S. and B.S. degrees from Cornell University. He has held a variety of positions in the Institute of Electrical and Electronics Engineers, has served as chairman of the U.S. Department of Commerce's Semiconductor Technology Advisory Committee, and currently chairs Working Group B of the Department of Defense's Advisory Group on Electron Devices.

ROBERT A. CHARPIE is chairman of Ampersand Ventures in Wellesley, Mass. Previously he served as president of Cabot Corporation, a chemicals, metals, and petroleum engineering organization; as president of Bell & Howell; and in a variety of positions with Union Carbide Corp., including director of the Reactor Division at Oak Ridge National Laboratory and president of the Electronics Division of Union Carbide. Charpie earned his B.S. with honors in 1948, his M.S. in 1949, and his D.Sc. in theoretical physics in 1950, all from the Carnegie Institute of Technology. He is a member of the National Academy of Engineering and a Fellow of the

American Physical Society, the American Nuclear Society, and the New York Academy of Sciences.

PHILIP M. CONDIT is the executive vice president, and general manager of the 777 Division, Boeing Commercial Airplane Group. In that capacity he supervises all work related to the development of a new airplane by the Group. During his years with Boeing, he has had assignments in sales, marketing, engineering, and production. Condit has a B.S. in mechanical engineering from the University of California, Berkeley; an M.S. in aeronautical engineering from Princeton University; and an M.S. in management from the Massachusetts Institute of Technology, where he was a Sloan Fellow. A member of the National Academy of Engineering, the Royal Aeronautical Society, and the Society of Automotive Engineers, Condit is a Fellow of the American Institute of Aeronautics and Astronautics.

ROBERT C. DEAN, JR., is the founder of five companies, including the company of which he is now president, Dean Technology, Inc. A recipient of B.S., M.S., and Sc.D. degrees from the Massachusetts Institute of Technology, he has extensive research and development experience in energy and bioprocessing systems. Dean is a member of the National Academy of Engineering and a Fellow of the American Society of Mechanical Engineers. He has ten U.S. patents and ten patent applications pending in mass cell culture and separation/purification for production of biopharmaceuticals.

RICHARD E. EMMERT was appointed executive director of the American Institute of Chemical Engineers in March 1988 following his retirement from Du Pont, where he was vice president for electronics, with worldwide responsibility for the company's electronic product businesses. He received his B.S. degree in chemical engineering from the University of Iowa and his M.S. and Ph.D. degrees, both in chemical engineering, from the University of Delaware. Emmert is a member of the National Academy of Engineering, the American Chemical Society, and the American Institute of Chemical Engineers, and has written technical articles for various engineering handbooks, journals, and other publications.

JOSEPH G. GAVIN, JR., is the retired president of Grumman Corporation, for which he has also served as a senior management consultant. He is a director of the American Association for the Advancement of Science and a Fellow of the American Astronautical Society and the American Institute of Aeronautics and Astronautics. Gavin was program director for the lunar module of the Apollo Project. He has been a member of the Department of Energy's Energy Research Advisory Board, and a member of several National Research Council committees. Gavin received B.S. and M.S. degrees in aeronautical engineering from the Massachusetts Institute of Technology. He is a member of the National Academy of Engineering.

JOHN W. LYONS is director of the National Institute of Standards and Technology and previously was the first director of that institution's National Engineering Laboratory. He has worked in various research and development positions at Monsanto Company and is the author of three books and has contributed to numerous other books, papers, and articles on technical or research topics. Lyons received his A.B. degree in chemistry from Harvard University and his A.M. and Ph.D. degrees in physical chemistry from Washington University. He is a member of the National Academy of Engineering and a Fellow of the American Association for the Advancement of Science and of the Washington Academy of Science.

WILLIAM F. MILLER is professor of public and private management and of computer science at Stanford University and president emeritus of SRI International. Miller received B.S., M.S., and Ph.D. degrees in physics from Purdue University. He is a member of the National Academy of Engineering and a Fellow of the American Academy of Arts and Sciences, the Institute of Electrical and Electronics Engineers, and the American Association for the Advancement of Science. He is a director of a number of business entities and a member of international advisory boards.

HAROLD G. SOWMAN has retired as corporate scientist from 3M company's Central Research Laboratories and Industrial & Electronic Sector Research Laboratory. He received B.S., M.S., and Ph.D. degrees in ceramic engineering from the University of Illinois. Sowman is a member of the National Academy of Engineering and a Fellow of the American Ceramic Society. The holder of thirty patents and author of more than twenty publications, he is recognized for his expertise in ceramics, especially high-temperature materials, "sol-gel" or "chemical ceramics," and ceramic fibers.

STUDY DIRECTOR

BRUCE R. GUILE is director of the Program Office of the National Academy of Engineering. In his seven years with the Academy, Guile has served as study director for numerous activities focused on industrial innovation, competitiveness, and technology policy related to both manufacturing and service industries. Before joining the Academy in 1984, Guile worked as research associate with the Berkeley Roundtable on the International Economy, and for several years with a management consulting firm. Guile holds a bachelor's degree in computer science and English literature from Heidelberg College, a Master of Public Policy from the University of Michigan, and a Ph.D. from the University of California, Berkeley.

Index